THE RUTH BANCROFT GARD

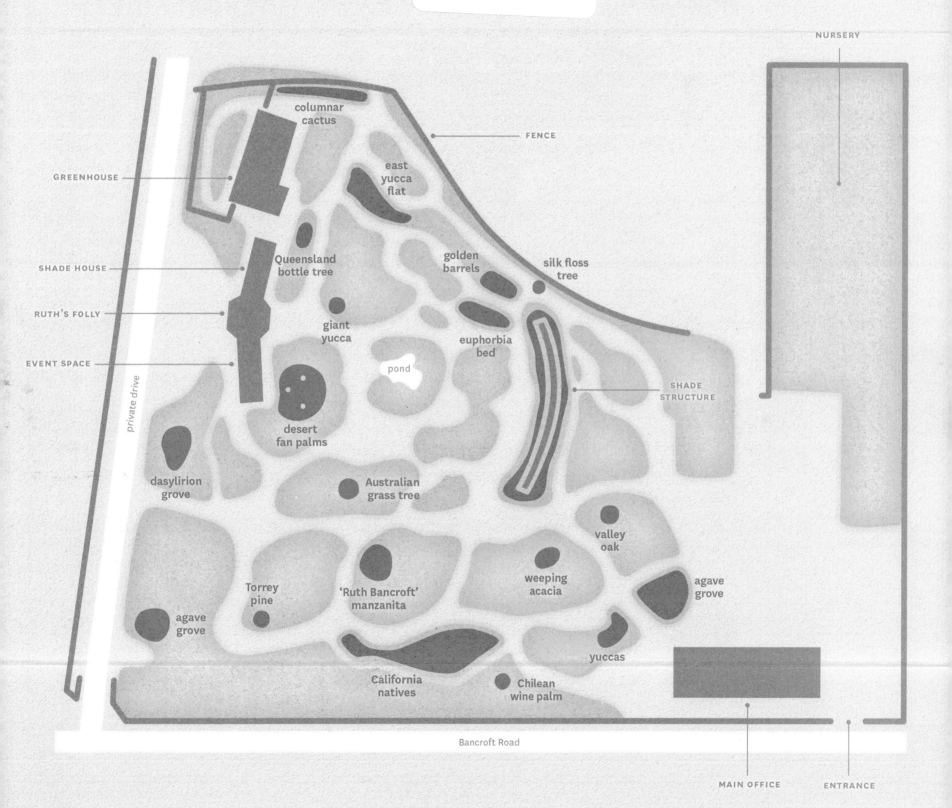

NURSERY

columnar cactus

FENCE

GREENHOUSE

east yucca flat

SHADE HOUSE

Queensland bottle tree

golden barrels

silk floss tree

RUTH'S FOLLY

giant yucca

euphorbia bed

EVENT SPACE

pond

SHADE STRUCTURE

private drive

desert fan palms

dasylirion grove

Australian grass tree

valley oak

weeping acacia

agave grove

Torrey pine

'Ruth Bancroft' manzanita

agave grove

yuccas

California natives

Chilean wine palm

Bancroft Road

MAIN OFFICE

ENTRANCE

THE
BOLD
DRY
GARDEN

THE BOLD DRY GARDEN

Lessons from
the Ruth Bancroft Garden

Johanna Silver
PHOTOGRAPHS BY MARION BRENNER

TIMBER PRESS | PORTLAND, OREGON

TO
RUTH

CONTENTS

FOREWORD

My childhood collection of bearded iris enlivened our small Michigan garden, but I struggled to maintain a collection of succulents in tiny pots on overly shaded windowsills. Upon moving to California in the late 1970s, I was thrilled to learn that both groups of plants thrived here. In old issues of *California Horticultural Society Journal*, I read of a magical garden in Walnut Creek filled with all sorts of shrubs, roses, and perennials (including a 200-foot-long border of bearded iris), as well as a two-acre succulent garden.

In 1979, my employer, Mai Arbegast, took me to see that garden and meet its creator, Ruth Bancroft. On a perfect day in late April, we arrived to find the bearded irises in full bloom and a stunning succulent garden bursting with color, textures, and exotic shapes (at least for this Midwesterner). I was in love—with both the garden and Ruth (who was, admittedly, older than my mother).

I talked about that garden to anyone who would listen, and began taking people to Walnut Creek to see it and to meet Ruth. Each semester-long plant-identification course I taught at UC Berkeley ended with a field trip to Ruth's garden, where I introduced the landscape architecture students to Ruth and to a bold and beautiful world of plants we scarcely had time to consider in class. I organized expeditions for members of the Strybing Arboretum Society to see this outstanding garden; even those who were disinclined toward succulents came away dazzled.

Frank Cabot was among those visitors. As a result of his first tour, he established the Garden Conservancy and encouraged his board of directors to choose Ruth's garden as its first sponsored garden. I worked alongside prominent Bay Area horticulturists, landscape architects, and educators to help the Conservancy and Ruth map out a strategy for turning her private garden into a public space.

As a member of the advisory board and, later, executive director for the Ruth Bancroft Garden, Inc., I had the pleasure of spending many hours with Ruth, gradually absorbing her vision for the garden and learning to appreciate the intellectual curiosity that guided its development.

A distinctly private person, Ruth created her garden for herself, but she was always happy to share it with others who were intrigued with her selection of plants. A major task of the Garden Conservancy was to spread the word about this seemingly secret garden to those who might benefit from its many messages: the value of texture and form over flowers, the dramatic compositions possible with big-and-bold forms, the diversity inherent in the world of succulents, and the important role these beautiful plants can play in water conservation for an arid (and drying) climate.

And now, Johanna Silver, the Ruth Bancroft Garden, Marion Brenner, and Timber Press have produced this magnificent book to enchant and educate even more garden enthusiasts with the story of this inspired plantswoman—and the brilliant garden she created.

Richard G Turner Jr
Editor emeritus, *Pacific Horticulture*

PREFACE

My Journey to Ruth's Garden

Yucca 'Bright Star' shines surrounded by *Tradescantia* 'Purple Heart', with a backdrop of Kenyan *Aloe kedongensis*. ▲

Before I started working on this book, I had never been to the Ruth Bancroft Garden. This was embarrassing for a garden editor at Sunset magazine to admit. Sure, I had heard of Ruth's garden. I knew it was a dry garden. I had seen photographs of the arching bed of tightly planted small succulents shielded by a shade structure and portraits of Ruth standing next to a patch of giant *Agave franzosinii*, but I had never visited. My first trip to this iconic garden was to be interviewed as a potential writer for this book.

My first impression of the garden was that it was small (it is 3 acres under cultivation). I wondered if there was enough for an entire book, if I would get bored, and if there was enough to photograph. Despite my hesitation, I was grateful for the opportunity, eager to immerse myself in the topic of dry gardening in the face of California's worst-ever drought, and excited about the chance to work with photographer Marion Brenner.

The year that followed was a crash course in Ruth's life, Ruth's plants, and Ruth's garden. It has been the ultimate humbling experience. The first thing I learned was that fancying us both "plant people" would not be enough to make me understand Ruth's drive. Ruth is a *collector*. I had no previous exposure to this subgroup, so I had to learn that more than just a love of plants motivates this population. Collectors have an insatiable need to possess knowledge, both intellectually and materially. Ruth's garden came from her desire to grow each and every plant that interested her (a list that never shrank) in order to learn each one fully. I quickly realized that while I might pass as succulent-literate to a beginner, Ruth's plant collection earns her extreme expert status, as her garden is a double black diamond of dry-adapted plants. Her "small" garden was too big and too full for me ever to fully grasp.

Many months into the project, it struck me that Marion—no stranger to shooting gardens large or small, foreign or domestic, natural or formal—had not once tired of Ruth's garden. She gleefully packed up her camera, tripod, and scrims and toted them out to Walnut Creek every weekend. Her enthusiasm deepened my interest. Marion, often bored by plant close-ups, could not get enough of them in Ruth's garden. Individual species were endlessly fascinating: the spiny, ornate cactus are curiously enticing, and their flowers are disproportionately delicate and dainty—an awesome foil to those spines. Marion and I obsessed over subtlety we had never known, like the metallic sheen on new opuntia growth that we spent almost

Agave parryi with pink leaf litter. ▲

Tall, columnar cactus frame a mysterious walkway. ▶

a full afternoon capturing. But Marion never tired of the vistas in the garden; I often had to holler at her to keep moving. Finally I acquiesced. Marion was right to linger, as the garden was always changing. The plants ebbed and flowed in their seasons of bloom and sleep. I expected year-round structure from cactus and succulents, but not the constant year-round change in growth and dormancy we encountered. We would arrive at the garden and try to walk around before setting up the camera, just to make sure we would not get so captivated by something near the entrance that we would never make it to the further reaches. Different things caught our eyes each time, from the tiniest ring of flowers that had developed along the crown of a cactus sitting at ground level to a freshly formed agave flower stalk that looked like a rocket about to propel into space. Ruth's garden boasts aloe plants in bloom from winter through summer, thanks to her longtime greenhouse manager, Brian Kemble, who has mastered a collection that is always giving. In spring, agaves swam amid a sea of orange- and yellow-flowered bulbine, but by early summer, ruby grass (*Melinis nerviglumis*) replaced the space between, adding movement and texture, with seed heads catching backlight.

Ruth and Brian.

The light was another dynamic factor. The garden grows in a flat stretch of low-lying suburbia, unimpeded by tall buildings, and is awash in constantly changing light that plays perfectly with all the plants, from the statuesque to the ephemeral. The glow softens in the afternoons and evenings, backlighting structural plants, peeking through strappy leaves, and making spines look like radiant auras. One evening, when I was sure I had seen it all, the large, drooping melaleuca branches caught the sun in a way I had never noticed. Its beauty paralyzed me. We had trouble walking away as we lost the light, and Marion increased the camera's exposure to see if we could capture one last shot.

Today I am no closer to being a plant collector than I was when I signed up to write this book. But a few things have changed. I will never again pretend to be literate with succulents (hearing someone loudly make that claim is your first indication to keep looking for a real expert). I am more lost than ever in a world of almost endless species, hybrids, and variations. But I am also fascinated by the details of plants, both as individual specimens and members of a

diverse planting. I cannot resist peering into the leaves of an eye-level palm so I can witness the gentle geometry of its leaves making room for one another to unfold unimpeded by the one before. If a haworthia is in a small pot, I will likely pick it up to see if I can catch its leaves' surreal translucent glow. And with a love of *Dyckia* fully realized, I do not plant a succulent mix without its dreamy sharp, radial structure as part of the composition. I am now more likely to research where a plant comes from and track down photos of its natural habitat in order to get a sense of what helps it thrive in the garden.

A love of plants is not what makes me feel connected to Ruth; rather, it is the practice of indulging my curiosity, as that is how she has spent her life. Intellectual as Ruth's love of plants might be, she retains a childlike curiosity. She is open to any plant type she finds appealing, from roses to cactus, and happy to talk with anyone, knowledgeable or not, about what they find appealing. You do not have to be an expert like Ruth to enjoy her garden. As long as you bring your curiosity, you are welcome inside her garden and into her world.

I started this book just after Ruth's 106th birthday and wrapped it up right before she turned 107. I met with her on several occasions in her home and once in the garden. While

Planted from one-gallon containers in the early 1970s, Ruth's trio of desert fan palms (*Washingtonia filifera*) looks exactly as it would in a desert oasis. Ruth was always a fan of a more natural look, so she left their grass skirts, which became part of their structural appeal.

her memory is understandably unreliable, she is very engaged with the world. She spends her days reading, listening to classical music and opera, and catching up on British dramas. When I first met her, I mentioned her recent birthday, and she swore there was no way she could have been 106. One sunny day we helped her into the garden because Brian was eager to show her recent updates. He gently oriented her to the history of a bed, updated her on the reasons behind particular choices, and asked for her approval. While they were staring at giant desert fan palms, he said, "You were planting the garden when you were in your sixties, and people said, 'It takes so long for these things to get big, you'll never live to see it.' But you did, and there they are. And they became magnificent." He reminded Ruth of her response: "You told them, 'Well, who cares if I'm around or not? Someone will be around. And if I don't plant it then nobody will get to see it.'"

During my time with Ruth, her eyes lit up twice: once on the subject of weeding ("I always felt like I was doing just a little bit of good in the world"), and once at the mention of Brian, who started working for her in 1980. Brian found a home for his horticultural obsessions in Ruth's garden, and a lifelong friend in Ruth. I interviewed many people and practically memorized Ruth's oral history, but I relied most on Brian for hard-hitting plant information and for understanding Ruth's intentions. He is a most trustworthy guide into her world.

I am honored to share Ruth's garden with you. And I hope you will find, like I did, that the longer you stare, the more there is to see. This is an opportune moment to reclaim our gardens as regionally appropriate spaces, and Ruth's is a treasure chest of inspiration, lessons learned, and beauty.

Johanna Silver

MEET RUTH

It was an accident that Ruth
became a pioneer of dry gardening

in the American West. Her lifelong love of plants—all of them, from wildflowers to roses—eventually led to an especially deep dive into cactus, succulents, and other dry-adapted plants from arid climates around the world. More than any other genre of plant she collected, the dry palette bit her the hardest. Her love affair started with a small rosette-shaped, fleshy-leaved aeonium. The architectural, ornately symmetrical forms of the genus stole her heart. And while she did not design her garden out of any desire to prove a point about water-wise gardening, their adaptations to dry conditions make these plants even more enchanting.

Ferocactus glaucescens, from eastern Mexico, has the bluest barrels, with matching yellow blooms and spines.

A DRY CLIMATE

Walnut Creek, California, has always been a dry-summer Mediterranean climate with no precipitation in the warmer months. The town's population boomed after the Second World War, when railroads, real estate developers, and municipalities sold California as a state of abundance filled with rich soil, sunshine, and water for everyone. Many believed it was a good thing that the state population was growing and that dams would be sufficient for providing enough water for farmers, industry, and residents. Concepts like drought or regionally appropriate landscaping were far from the mainstream consciousness. As suburban development closed in on her husband's historic family farm with single-family homes and green lawns, Ruth unintentionally created a model of dry gardening on the little patch of land they still possessed.

California residents are waking up with what feels like a collective hangover from the idea of turf as status quo, which is a long-outdated metric of affluence. We are becoming aware of just how wasteful our landscapes are. California is the only Mediterranean climate–region in the world in which lawns are the norm, and these could not be more of a regional mismatch, as the grass needs regular irrigation during the season when no rain falls. The figures are stark. As much as 70 percent of the water flowing to California's cities and suburbs is used to support gardens and outdoor features. The typical suburban lawn in California uses as much as 45,000 gallons of water per year to irrigate front and back yards, plus regular inputs of synthetic fertilizers and gas-powered mowers.

Yet we need our home gardens more than ever. New research suggests that the cultivated parts of suburbia actually support a surprisingly large amount of biological diversity that is otherwise losing its habitat. But it is critical that we cultivate a space in sync with our regional

The bright blooming candelabra of an *Aloe* hybrid
(*A. ferox* × *A. arborescens*).

environment. It is time to act as stewards rather than conquerors, and to understand that our yards and gardens are part of the natural environment, not distinct from it.

Long before this wake-up call (and without even knowing it), Ruth created a dynamic garden that responded to the logic of place. She constructed an ecologically sound garden and rehabilitated land that decades of ranching had compacted and decimated. The Great Depression forced Ruth to abandon her dreams of becoming an architect, but she was able to use her innate design skills in her garden. From spirals to rosettes, silver-green leaves to sharp spines, the dry plant palette is bold, structural, and anything but understated. Ruth has proven that a xeric garden can be lush, welcoming, and full of hidden nooks and views—exactly what we are thirsty for in this changing climate.

Ruth was fearless in her approach to gardening. Although she nearly lost her entire collection to a freak cold spell the first winter it was in the ground, she started over immediately—but never played it safe with her choices. She had a strong case of zone denial; an unwill-ingness to be limited by a few degrees of cold. She tried anything she fancied, and went to great lengths to protect plants during winter.

In addition to horticultural experimentation, this special plot of land also represents the first of its kind in garden preservation for the United States. While Ruth was content growing the garden just for herself, Frank Cabot, one of the world's leading garden preservationists, had the foresight to recognize the space as uniquely American and worth protecting. In 1989, he established the Garden Conservancy, which is devoted to preserving unique and noteworthy private gardens and helping them convert to public ones. As of 2015 the organization has helped save or restore more than 80 gardens, and Ruth's was its very first.

Ruth and her mother, circa 1909. ▶

Ruth as a toddler, circa 1911. ▲

RUTH'S EARLY YEARS

To call Ruth Bancroft a gardener is the understatement of a lifetime. Although she gardened diligently for decades, it was simply a means to an end on a lifelong quest for knowledge. Ruth is blessed, or perhaps cursed, with intellectual curiosity that is satisfied only when she accumulates something in its entirety. For Ruth, to collect is to know—to study, record, and preserve. Along the way, she was able to learn, travel, and design without leaving her own yard. And she built one of the most impressive collections of dry-adapted plants on the planet, all for the sake of knowing and marveling at the natural world.

Ruth always loved plants. Born in 1908 to Swedish immigrants, Ruth Petersson moved from Boston to Northern California as an infant when her father was offered a job as a professor of Latin at the University of California, Berkeley (UC Berkeley). Every time her mother pushed her in the carriage, Ruth insisted on carrying a yellow flower during the ride. Once she grew out of the buggy, she explored the largely undeveloped hills of North Berkeley, admiring wildflowers like delicate, white-blooming *Trillium*, showy pink-flowered currant (*Ribes*), and blue- or white-flowered soap lily (*Chlorogalum*). She even dug up small plants to replant in her own backyard, showing the innate confidence she brought to gardening later in life.

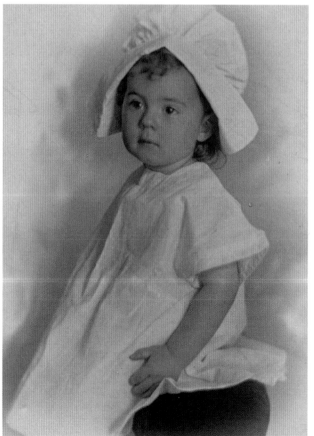

Young Ruth posing with a parasol. ◄

A page from a book Ruth enjoyed as a child. ▼

Ruth adored books in equal measure, a testament to her desire to learn. Her first favorite was a German book called *When the Root Children Wake Up* (*Etwas Von Den Wurzelkindern*), by Sibylle von Olfers, which features a parade of children carrying stems with different flowers on top. Ruth loved that image and spent ample time examining the variations among the blooms.

Und als der Frühling
kommt ins Land,
da ziehn gleich einem
bunten Band,
die Käfer, Blumen,
Gräser klein,
frohlockend in die
Welt hinein.

Young, curious Ruth. On the back of the photo, Ruth's shaky writing reads, "Ruth. Five years old?" ▲

Ruth, circa 1913, studious from the start. ◄

Berkeley was the perfect cross-section of intellectualism and a mild climate—an ideal environment for breeding horticulture enthusiasts. Ruth shared her neighborhood with two noteworthy iris breeders who fostered her budding tendencies toward plant collecting. Sydney B. Mitchell, founder of the American Iris Association, and Carl Salbach, a great iris breeder of the 1940s, both spent time with Ruth and taught her about bearded iris culture. This was a great first plant for Ruth. Irises are generally carefree and generous with their flowers, and they provided a wonderful array of shades to catch her attention.

Ruth's penchant for thrifty collecting began early, as these generous breeders gave her iris rhizomes to plant in her fledgling home garden. As a little girl, she did not have money to buy plants, but she acquired things, in her words, "one way or another," and found great satisfaction in seeing plants grow and bloom.

Before he was the father of modern California landscape architecture, Thomas "Tommy" Church lived in Berkeley near Ruth's school. Tommy, six years older than Ruth, showed her his flower garden at his mother's home, which included enormous dahlias. Tommy graduated with a degree in

Ruth, likely in her twenties. ◄
A portrait of Ruth, undated. ►

landscape architecture from UC Berkeley in 1922, and he went on to become a pioneer in developing a type of garden design known as California Style. Although Ruth and Tommy did not cross paths again later in life, their childhoods indicate what a great time it was to be a plant lover in Berkeley.

Six years on Thomas Church's tail, Ruth enrolled in UC Berkeley in 1926, planning to study architecture. She really wanted landscape architecture, but the program was new, and her parents steered her onto the more traditional architecture path. In a program of 50 students, Ruth was one of two women. Three years later, the stock market crashed and Ruth was forced to abandon her career ambitions: "None of the men could get architecture jobs. And of course there were very few girls studying it then. So I decided to go into teaching, which was safe." Ruth graduated with a teaching certificate in 1932 and taught home economics at a school in Merced, although she was less than passionate about the curriculum, particularly cooking. Decades elapsed before her penchant for landscape design had a chance to bloom in her dry garden.

Ruth married into a prestigious family. Seen here, historian Hubert Howe Bancroft, Philip Bancroft Sr., and young Philip Jr., whom Ruth later married.

In the mid-1930s, Ruth went on a blind date with her future husband, Philip Bancroft Jr., a friend of her sister's boyfriend. Although he was not an obsessive collector like Ruth, the two connected deeply around a shared love of art, books, classical music, and opera. (Phil did have a small hat collection, acquired during childhood travels with his mother.)

Ruth had met a man with prestigious roots. Phil's grandfather, Hubert Howe Bancroft, was the child of abolitionist parents, and his childhood home in Granville, Ohio, was a stop along the Underground Railroad. In 1852, at the height of the Gold Rush, Hubert moved to San Francisco to open a regional branch of his brother's book-publishing business. He eventually devoted all of his efforts to being a historian and writer, and he published a 39-volume history of the American West. He amassed a library so large that UC Berkeley bought it in 1905 and named it in his honor. In the 1880s, Hubert moved his family 30 miles east of San Francisco to a 400-acre ranch in Walnut Creek with towering Mount Diablo in the distance. Eventually the land had to pay for itself, so Hubert planted hundreds of acres of Bartlett pears and walnuts. It was a successful operation, winning first place in the state for pears for almost a decade in the 1930s. At the height of production, the farm employed 200 seasonal workers, and shipped pears to the eastern United

States and as far as England. It remained a productive orchard through the late 1960s, when the city rezoned the property to be residential. The Ygnacio Valley underwent a rapid change from rural to suburban, and all but 11 acres of land were sold to developers eager to expand in Walnut Creek. It was passed down to Hubert's son, Philip Bancroft, and eventually to Philip Jr.

Phil attended Harvard, studying literature and art. After graduation, he returned home and assumed the helm of the family's Bartlett orchard. Despite his distinguished roots and penchant for fine arts, Phil was a farmer with a sense of humor. After they married on June 30, 1939, he arrived in his manure truck to gather Ruth and her belongings from her parents' home in Berkeley. When Ruth objected to the vehicle, Phil responded, "Well, I washed it out!"

Phil moved Ruth to his family's farm. When she arrived, the Bancroft farm had already been in the family for more than a half century. Phil's parents were overbearing and judgmental, and they never fully warmed up to Ruth. Phil's mother was insulted that Ruth added a water softener in her house, and she looked down on Ruth for having a number of miscarriages before carrying a pregnancy to term. It did not help that Ruth and Phil lived directly next door to his parents. As an escape, Ruth took to gardening in the beds surrounding the home, called the Swiss Chalet for its loose resemblance to an alpine house. She filled the garden with bright flowers, perhaps in an effort to brighten up the dark mood of the family compound.

Ruth and Phil enjoying a social gathering at their home.

Ruth and Phil were the best of friends. She loved his ability to jump into anything, be it carpentry, plumbing, or a broken car, and figure it out. Phil doted on Ruth and was eager to please her. Eventually they had three children—Peter, Nina, and Kathy. Phil farmed, and Ruth was responsible for cooking, cleaning, and raising the family. For the duration of their decades-long romance, they held season tickets to the San Francisco Opera and frequented the symphony in San Francisco and Walnut Creek. Opera was always blaring in the home, and the opera from the Met was broadcast loudly on Sundays.

Ruth also loved listening to a radio show that featured young, classically trained artists.

By the mid-1950s, Philip Sr. had passed away, and the couple and their three children moved into the property's main house to live with Ruth's mother-in-law. The home is an eclectic American-style compound measuring about 4000 square feet. Ruth made some changes, including creating a sun porch, a driveway, a larger kitchen, and a proper dining room. The house remains largely untouched since the 1950s, with mint green kitchen cabinetry and counters, mid-20th-century furniture, and art on every wall.

Ruth and her family pose in the late 1960s. Behind her are Peter and Phil. Next to her, from left to right, are daughters Nina and Kathy.

Despite her experience as a home economics teacher, Ruth did not much like cooking. But she was a dutiful housewife and got the job done, including preparing lunch for the farm crew every day. And in any of those tasks— gardening, cooking, taking care of the home—Ruth's propensity to collect was ever present. She kept an archive of thousands of handwritten recipes in custom-made kitchen drawers, filed according to a robust system of categorization. First she sorted according to the type of dish: salad, side, main, dessert, and so on. Then she marked the number of people the dish could serve, whether dinner alone with Phil, an easy lunch for the crew, or big meal for a larger house party. She made notes of where she found the best ingredients, whether in her garden or from a certain market. Finally, accompanying each and every recipe was a note marking its original source and a grade of its success in her cooking rotation (X equaled good and XX meant very good).

Ruth at the beach with her son, Peter, shells in her hand. ▲

Shells rest gently on a bed of cotton. ◄

COLLECTING: A FAMILY AFFAIR

Either by nurture or nature, Ruth passed along her love of collecting to all three of her children (and most of her grandchildren). Peter gathered butterflies from childhood into adulthood, pinning them to boards and making sure each one was properly labeled, just like Mom would have done. Nina collects ceramic horse models and antiques, particularly demitasse cups, individual pepper shakers, and salt dishes. Kathy is hooked on Native American jewelry, beads, fabric, cloisonné, and Foo Dogs (Chinese guardian lions).

There is a certain flavor of obsession that comes with collecting, an inability to stop. A collector is passionate, driven, and on a quest for knowledge. The habit only intensifies as the desired objects become more obscure. Collectors, by definition, develop discerning taste (which often exceeds budget). Ruth is the rare collector who also keeps meticulously organized records. She took such good care of everything she gathered and left such a robust paper trail that she is

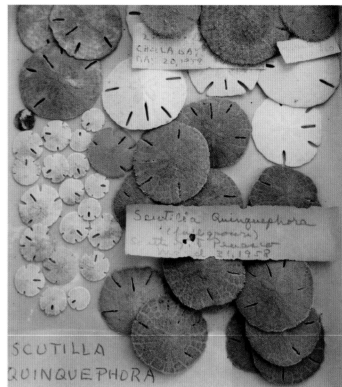

Shells found on San Quentin Beach in 1959. ▲

Sand dollars in shades of brown, white, and pale blue. ▼

still able to share everything she learned. In the garden, every plant is accounted for—where it came from, how it performed each year, and what maintenance it requires to stay happy.

Ruth also amassed art, books, and textiles, but her two most noteworthy collections—plants and seashells—tapped into her love of the outdoors. While raising three young children in the 1950s, Ruth developed a springtime ritual. Each March, when the storms were most fierce and the tides were lowest, Ruth and Phil tossed Peter, Nina, and Kathy into the family station wagon and headed for Pescadero, where the family owned a tiny cabin and camped outside in a large canvas army surplus tent. In the early morning, sometimes with Peter and Nina in tow, Ruth drove to nearby beaches to gather shells, crabs, sea stars, sand dollars, and anything else she could find. Ruth taught her children the names of all the sea creatures, as well as the tricks of collecting. (For example, if you want to get a

limpet [an aquatic snail] off a rock, you have to surprise it by getting the knife under it right away or it will clamp down.) Back at the cabin, Ruth lit the stove, placed a large pot on top, and boiled the bounty to kill off any living (and therefore perishable) components—and caused the cabin to become quite fragrant.

Sometimes the journeys were further from home. Occasionally the family traveled to Mexico for shell-collecting adventures. One year they went to Puerto Peñasco, then a small fishing village, in the state of Sonora. In the motel room, Nina watched her mother boil the shells on the miniature burner she'd brought along. Ruth flattened and bound sea stars and chitons onto boards tied with string to prevent them from rolling up.

After each trip, Ruth spread her acquisitions across a table and pored over her collection of books in order to identify and label (in Latin, of course) her findings. She placed each type in its own flat cardboard box (from an old

Ruth's friends and family were shocked when they realized the volume of shells preserved in boxes.

puzzle or a pair of hosiery) lined with a layer of cotton, along with a handwritten label that specified the month and year she gathered it, as well as the beach on which she found it.

After years upon years of these springtime journeys, Ruth amassed a huge amount of perfectly preserved sea creatures. Phil, always eager to please Ruth, built custom shelves in an upstairs room for her to store her shells.

The collection sat untouched for decades. Around 2012, Becky Rice Harrington, former executive director of Ruth's garden, decided to take a look. It was vaster than she had ever imagined, and she phoned the California Academy of

Sciences to inquire about any interest. Ruth had so pristinely preserved and recorded the sea life that the Academy took tens of thousands to become part of its archives, including species that are now extinct.

Ruth was captivated with strong forms in nature. The geometry of the shells was a precursor to her love for cactus and succulents, as the vast majority of both collections feature round forms with striking detail. She had quietly and single-handedly collected and preserved enough to create her own mini museum. And her meticulous approach to collecting plants would be her greatest triumph.

Ruth's home is surrounded by gardens. Here her rose collection still blooms in vibrant colors, while her first *Cereus* cactus stands tall in the distance.

OBSESSED WITH PLANTS

From her earliest memories of exploring the hills of Berkeley to her annual beach trips, Ruth loved being outside, and she was completely consumed by natural forms. From spines to flowers, nothing grabbed Ruth's attention as much as plants. Long before she got her hands on succulents, nearby horticulturalists were familiar with her other collections. From her first years in the Swiss Chalet, she filled beds outside the home with as much blooming color as would fit. After the renovations to the main house, Ruth turned her attention to the gardens immediately surrounding the home.

Ruth and Phil hired Ted Osmundson, a landscape architect who had collaborated with Thomas Church. Ted was accustomed to working in the more immediate Bay Area, specifically Oakland. He saw the shade of the magnificent oak trees on the Bancroft property and recommended planting camellias, rhododendrons, and azaleas. Ruth had been gardening for a few years in Walnut Creek, and she knew the climate was significantly different from Oakland. It was much hotter in the summer and much colder in the winter, the soils were heavy clay, and the water was very alkaline. Ruth noted that Ted's choices were not suitable for her space. He ignored her suggestions—either because of arrogance or refusal to listen to a woman—and within a year all his plantings were dead. Ruth took over the planting beds and experimented with mixed perennials. She soon had collections of hybrid tea and shrub roses, daffodils, and scented pelargoniums. As with everything else, Ruth paid attention to what worked and what did not, and she kept detailed records. She did not just want to make things pretty; she wanted to learn.

Ruth's iris in bloom.

possible on everything that fascinated her. She developed her own library of texts on plants and shells. She also wrote down every plant she purchased, where she planted it, how she cared for it, and how it performed. She even kept track of her daily garden tasks (every plant planted, every weed pulled), logging everything into spiral journals that filled their own filing cabinet. Each year she evaluated and made changes so she could continually improve the iris display. Ruth continued to plant, record, and refine the iris collection well into her nineties. While Ruth is famous for her dry garden, her iris collection was the first to earn her notoriety because of its breadth of cultivars. Every spring, iris enthusiasts stop by to snap pictures and take notes. It is a wonderful historical record of hybrid bearded iris.

Ruth collected plants to satisfy her own curiosity. She desired no fame, fortune, or notoriety. When she established the dry garden with her first drought-tolerant plants in the early 1950s, she was not particularly concerned about water conservation. The plants simply fascinated her, and she wanted to get to know all of them. She took cues from her climate and was willing to experiment and fail. Over the years, she developed confidence in her decisions about what to plant. Similarly, while Ruth appreciated the beauty of any flower, she was content to leave them in the garden as part of the collection. Nothing made it inside as a cut flower. Becky Rice Harrington was outside with Ruth one day during the spring iris flush. There was a bent stem lying in the driveway, topped with a perfect blossom. Becky snipped it and told Ruth she would put it in some water. Ruth told Becky she could have it. Cut flowers were not the point. Ruth was not into the seashells for any one shell, the iris for any one bloom, or the succulents for any one fleshy leaf. They were all merely pieces of the whole, opportunities to learn about diversity in the natural world.

If all of this makes her sound dreadfully serious, know that Ruth loves to laugh. She has a mischievous sparkle in her eye when she smiles, and she is quick to giggle. She is a straight shooter, direct to the point of almost being blunt, and happiest when in the garden or otherwise absorbed in something she loves. She and Phil were longtime birders, and occasionally joined the local Audubon chapter for

Ruth's childhood introduction to the iris world left quite an impression, and by the early 1950s she had a significant collection of her own. Irises are a great choice for the Walnut Creek climate. They are very well adapted to dry summers, and they can tolerate the heavy clay soils. Ruth planted a sweep of her long wraparound driveway in bearded irises representing nearly every height, bloom size, and color of the rainbow. A cascade of flowers appeared for nearly six weeks each spring. Ruth followed care instructions to a tee. Iris rhizomes need to be dug and divided every three years, so she dug and divided one-third of the collection each year. It took a month of working full time to divide and replant her collection, but the results were magnificent.

And whenever there was an opportunity to keep records, Ruth did. Her paper trail deserves its own fame. In her small office, she kept newspaper clippings of plants she liked and years' worth of catalogs that filled entire filing drawers. There were also tons of books, as Ruth wanted to read as much as

Ruth among her iris collection in September 2005. ◄

Iris along either side of Ruth's driveway. ▼

Sunday bird-watching outings. But Ruth had two complaints. First, the birders were too serious. She disliked that they shushed everyone and were not interested in any talk whatsoever. Second, they cared only about the birds, while Ruth was also fascinated with the trees. She wanted to know which species of tree supported what kind of wildlife and how the two related. Ruth was always connecting dots, looking at the interactions between pieces, and curious about nature—without an agenda beyond learning.

THE BEGINNING OF THE DRY GARDEN

As Ruth's gardens and family grew,
a dramatic plant type other than
iris caught her eye—succulents.

Ruth clipped articles about these sculptural drought-tolerant plants, not widely available then, long before she procured a living one for herself. Perfectly preserved in her records is a 1937 *Family Circle* with an opuntia on the cover, along with several *San Francisco News* articles. One from September 13, 1940, by Louise Weick, begins, "Succulents, one of the most fascinating tribes of plants for indoor culture, have become immensely popular in recent years. They appeal particularly to persons who appreciate the whimsicalities and curiosities of plant life rather than the usual show-offiness of flowers."

Ruth spent the next decade patiently snipping and saving any tidbit of information about these plants, even though she did not yet own one. In the 1950s, she and a friend went to the estate sale of a woman named Glenn Davidson. They were hunting for antique furniture, but when passing the garden, Ruth spotted a rosette-shaped aeonium. She purchased a few of these small hybrids (named *Aeonium* 'Glenn Davidson', as the furniture seller had also done her own breeding), and her dry plant collection was born.

Ruth's very first succulent, *Aeonium* 'Glenn Davidson', still lives in her garden. ▲

Ariocarpus, a small type of Mexican cactus with dense clumps of white wool stemming from its center, grows in the propagation greenhouse. The plant is cold tolerant but dislikes winter rain, so the greenhouse is the safest spot for it. ▶

FALLING IN LOVE WITH CACTUS AND SUCCULENTS

Ruth, always on the quiet side, shied away from hyperbole when asked why she loves these plants: "It was just the form that I liked." But it is easy to see what she admires about this horticultural eye candy. Some have such remarkable symmetry that it seems impossible that they have sprung from soil. Many are prickly enough to cause serious injury, but then burst open in the most conspicuous, come-hither Day-Glo blooms. Hailing from parts of the world where water is in short supply, their moisture-saving adaptations are mind boggling, from modified stems, leaves, and bases that store moisture to spines that deter predators and reflect sun (Brian noted that the meaner the plant, the more Ruth liked it). Some plants adapt to resemble polished pebbles or old rocks, seemingly more mineral than plant, and others thicken their skin to be unpalatable to grazers. These delicate beasts represent beauty from some of the most dry and hostile locations on the planet.

From those first aeoniums, Ruth's interest could not be checked. She approached the plants with meticulous record keeping and deep curiosity. She worked in themes, starting

Aeonium collected in an old shade house.

with rosette-shaped succulents (*Aeonium*, *Agave*, *Aloe*, *Echeveria*, and terrestrial bromeliads) and moving on to cactus. All her plants were small specimens kept in terra-cotta pots. After purchasing a plant, she learned every possible thing about the genus, made a list of her favorites (which never reached completion), worked on acquiring them, and repeated the process again and again.

Ruth's collection quickly grew too large for the small glass-paned greenhouse outside her home. Phil built a series of wood and corrugated plastic shade houses, which turned into a maze of structures still standing today (in various conditions), each filled with carefully sorted and labeled collections of genera within the succulent world.

Ruth was eager to see how these plants would fare in the ground, too, so she began planting them just outside her home. When they promptly died, she knew from the signs of rot that drainage had been an issue. She dug up small patches of earth and created mounds, her earliest experiments in mitigating the clay soil to be more amenable to these dry-adapted plants that thrive on good drainage.

Collecting these plants in the 1950s and '60s was not easy. This was not the era of readily available echeverias and sedums at home-improvement stores and supermarkets. There were no Internet searches or Pinterest boards. These plants were hard to come by, and Ruth had the most luck in Southern California. She and Phil made occasional visits to Borrego Springs, and they visited nurseries—including Johnson's Cactus Gardens in Paramount—and filled the station wagon to the brim on the way back. Locally, Berkeley Horticultural Nursery, in business since 1922, occasionally carried cactus and succulents, but The Dry Garden in Oakland did not become a resource until 1987. Ruth's logs include many nurseries that have since gone out of business, including Lila's Nursery in San Rafael.

Copiapoa on shelves in the greenhouse. This genus, notable for chalky white bodies and black spines, comes from northern Chile, a region with almost zero rainfall but abundant summer fog.

Ruth's original cactus, *Cereus hildmannianus*, stands adjacent to the series of greenhouses that Phil built for her growing collection.

Plant collectors—people as deeply steeped in acquisition as Ruth—often become explorers, traveling far and wide to see their loves in their natural habitat (*in situ*, as they call it), and possibly collect seeds (legally or illegally) to plant at home. Ruth was not a traveler. Aside from one trip to Europe with a friend after college and occasional visits to Southern California, she stayed in Northern California. But her years of diligent research have lent her a vast amount of knowledge about geography. It is as though she traveled via her many plant catalogs when she stayed up late and pored over her options.

The former orchard, trees removed, with the beginnings of irrigation ditches for Ruth's garden. ▶

The beginnings of the garden. Note the iris collection along the driveway with no fence between her home garden and the new dry one. ▼

Taken from the roof of the folly, this 1973 shot reveals the garden in its infancy, unfenced from Bancroft Road, with no housing development to the east.

FROM GREENHOUSE TO GROUND

In 1971, all but 11 acres of the original 400 of the farm had been sold to developers, and the very last of the walnut orchard on the Bancroft property was cut down. The trees were sick with blackline, a soil-borne fungal disease. Suddenly Phil had three acres on his hands—just a giant patch of flat, bare soil, not in the best health after years of monoculture and disking.

By this point, Ruth was 63 years old and had three grown children. Many would have considered themselves ready for retirement, or at least allowed themselves to slow down, but not Ruth. She was just getting started. Something was stirring deep inside her. Her succulent collection now numbered more than 2000 small potted plants stored in shade houses and greenhouses erected close to the main house. She hand watered her entire assemblage with a hose or a little sprinkler attached to the end of the hose. Phil thought that planting the garden into beds with existing irrigation systems might save her some time, so he offered up the newly cleared acreage. Little did he know that no matter what went into the ground, Ruth would always be acquiring more, and those shelves would never be empty. But with that offer, she started planning and planting her masterpiece.

There was one condition to the new garden: Phil would dig no new wells, and they would not tap into city water. While he was not a conservationist, Phil had a keen sense of resource use on the farm, and he knew the existing well water had to continue to supply the entire family compound and accompanying gardens. Ruth understood that the plants would need perfect drainage and mostly dry conditions, and she was up for the challenge. Thus the Bancrofts began practicing voluntary water restrictions in the very early 1970s. This coalescence of dry plants and no additional water was key in laying the foundation for what would become an incredible resource to the community.

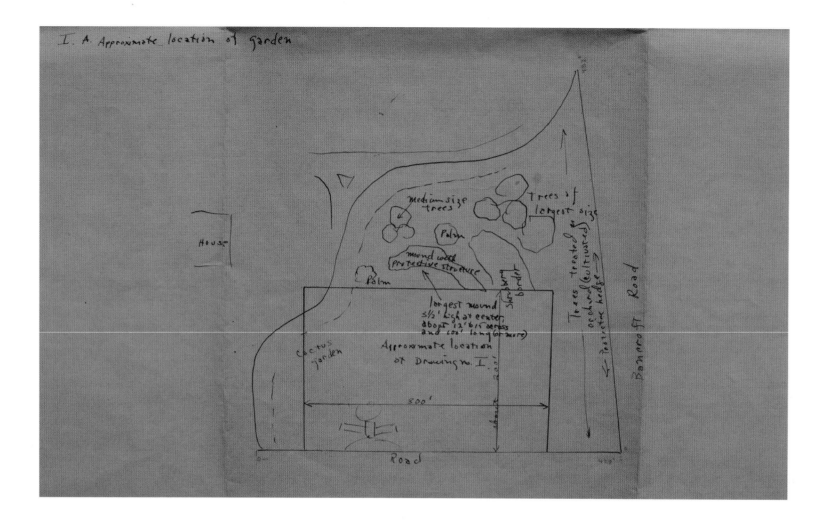

I. A. Approximate location of garden

House

Medium size trees

Trees of largest size

Palm

mound with protective structure

Palm

largest mound 5½' high at center, about 12' 6/5 across and 100' long (or more)

Shrub border

Trees treated orchard (cultivated)

Protective hedge

Bancroft Road

cactus garden

Approximate location of Drawing no. I

800'

sidewalk

Road

420'

Although she had meticulously designed the gardens around her home, including the famous iris collection, Ruth called in help for laying out her tiny dry-adapted plants in a three-acre space. She hired Lester Hawkins, famed designer and co-owner of Western Hills Nursery in Occidental, Sonoma County. Lester had a good reputation, and people regarded him as an innovative designer. It is noteworthy that Ruth, so competent with gardening and so opinionated about what she liked, felt "incapable," in her words, of designing the dry garden. While she clearly identified as a gardener, she did not consider herself a designer—a career field that men then dominated (and still do).

With informal freehand sketches, Lester shaped the overall flow of the garden to comprise mounded planting islands surrounded by meandering paths. It was perfect for viewing the collection from various angles, allowing Ruth to compose miniature compositions of plant groups to consider her studies. This series of undulating mounds added important topographical interest to an otherwise large, flat piece of land. Lester approached the mounds from an aesthetic viewpoint, but from her experiments Ruth knew the islands would be key to fixing the clay soil and providing more drainage. Lester also insisted on a centrally placed pond as a counterpoint to the plants. Most of Ruth's dry-adapted plants originate in deserts, where water is incredibly precious. In such a harsh environment, water is an oasis, an important element that supports life itself.

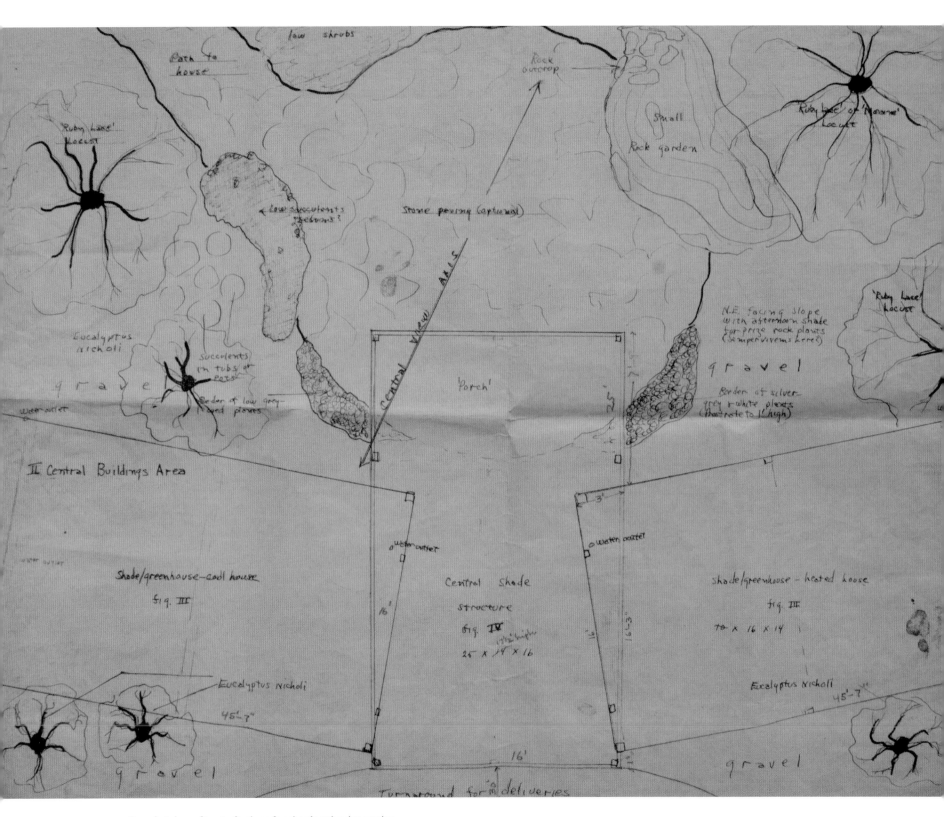

Two sketches of Lester's plans for shaping the dry garden.

Ruth and Phil at work filling the pond. The pond planted (above right) and the view as Lester intended (opposite), straight through the garden from the pond oasis (just out of sight in the foreground).

Working with Lester was amusing, albeit overwhelming. He had seemingly endless energy, and Ruth always had to have a fresh pot of coffee on hand per his request. Lester was also erratic: Ruth found him planting trees, his one main botanical contribution, haphazardly. She once caught him planting a palm tree and a locust 2 feet apart. While she appreciated the input Lester offered—the islands, the wide paths, and the pond—Ruth seemed to take pride in the fact that most of the plants with which he arrived died promptly.

Although the garden eventually evolved to become a more designed space, it began as a collector's showpiece—a place for Ruth to keep learning about her diverse, varied plants. She was not trying to design a masterpiece or follow the rules that accomplished landscape architect Thomas Church promoted: unity, function, simplicity, and scale. Ruth, overwhelmed at the acreage available for her small plants (nothing was in a container larger than a gallon), just needed a home for her collection. Creating smaller beds allowed her to treat each one as a separate entity, far easier to tackle than three bare acres. Every bed received a number or label, and this system is still in use. When Ruth first planted the garden, she did her best to pay attention to vistas and overall cohesion, but no bed necessarily related to the one next to it. Each composition was an opportunity to explore a characteristic, a genus, or even a color.

Paths, as important as the planting beds, are always at least 3 feet wide, allowing ample room for visitors to move throughout the garden. From the beginning, Ruth was clear that she did not want hard edges between plants and beds. She preferred room for the plants to billow over their borders, an especially important feature because of the many spines in her collection. In addition to sectioning the acreage into smaller-size design projects, the meandering pathways also allow passersby to see each composition from all angles. They are perfect platforms for showing off a collection.

Ruth's folly under construction in September 1973, the finished folly, and standing tall and surrounded by plants in 1976.

Many of the original trees came from Lester's nursery. They provided shade for the succulents that do better with some protection from full sun. Lester used what he had on hand in his inventory instead of acquiring trees specifically intended to fit in with Ruth's garden. However, some of his selections have persisted as important features, including the conifers surrounding the pond. At first glance, one might think these needled evergreens have no place among cactus and succulents, but some conifers are extremely drought tolerant, having adapted to withstand decimating dry air and frozen soil. Their aggressive root systems allow them to tap into moisture reserves deep below, and their waxy needle leaves limit the surface area exposed to evaporation. Like many succulents, a waxy bloom covers their leaves, further sealing in moisture. In Ruth's garden, a Rocky Mountain pinyon pine (*Pinus edulis*), single-leaf pinyon pine (*P. monophylla*), and Rocky Mountain bristlecone pine (*P. aristata*) stand guard by the pond.

Ruth got additional help from an architect friend, Ken Householder, to design her dream of having a folly at the entrance to the garden. She had always wanted a structure to connect the two shade houses that Phil erected in 1972. A folly—an English term from the 18th and 19th centuries that describes a whimsical structure in a garden—connects the two structures, creating a grand entrance. Ruth's folly, a mint green Art Nouveau gazebo, still stands as an iconic part of the garden.

Ruth and Lester spent months amending the heavy clay soil, which was severely compacted from decades of agricultural disking. This patch of land was the most unlikely place to plant a desert garden. Xerophytic plants, which have adapted to pass their life cycle and thrive despite drought, cannot tolerate standing water and compact soil. Lester brought in truckloads of moss rock, a dark rock with pockmarks that was (and is) the most common type sold at landscaping yards. They created planting islands, each one composed of an undulating, mounded raised bed that served as a canvas for Ruth.

Ruth's original planting beds, built up with rock to mitigate the heavy clay soil of Walnut Creek. Here, Ruth tucked *Dudleya* into rock crevices, just as it grows in its native California and Mexico.

Ruth's young garden in 1973, with an arching shade structure protecting shade-loving succulents.

SMALL PLANTS

As in her childhood, Ruth was thrifty in her plant acquisition. She never spent money on larger plants or boxed trees. "I'd never get a five-gallon can," she recalled with pride, "occasionally a gallon, but usually the smaller containers." Granted, the small containers were more commonly available in those days (and Ruth could fit much more into her car on her yearly pilgrimages to Southern California), but she also found that they grew faster when planted in the ground and caught up with anything from a larger pot.

Even without any concern about money or availability, Ruth likely would have opted for small plants. Having only small containers allowed her to watch a plant grow from its juvenile stage to its mature size, which is not possible if you buy only big specimens. Ruth scrutinized her collections and chose the best forms of each variety to put in the ground. She was a patient perfectionist, willing to wait until she had many forms from which to choose.

When it came time to plant the three acres of freshly mounded land, the plants (including palm trees, a silver-blue cycad, and yuccas) were in 4- or 6-inch containers and the occasional gallon. Ruth researched every plant and left room for it to reach its eventual size, unless she could not track down that information, in which case she estimated. This was quite a challenge. Most of Ruth's collection was glacially slow growing, maturity was decades away, and she was working with a group of plants that no one else in the area was cultivating. "She didn't have a lot of firsthand exposure to what these plants would look like in a garden setting," said longtime friend Dick Turner. "She wrote letters and read books. Can you envision laying them out and trying to visualize what they would grow into? She had to have a great imagination."

It is hard to conceive of being content to plant an entire collection in the ground and unveil nothing more than tiny plants, but Ruth's patience and thorough planning allowed the garden to grow into a masterpiece, with each plant taking a star turn. Ruth took the long view when she planted. She was more interested in watching her collection grow than creating an instant garden. It looked pathetically sparse, but just shy of 50 years later, she has some of most impressive specimens of their kind, from towering *Yucca filifera* to the patch of *Agave franzosinii* to the grove of *Washingtonia filifera* planted in a cluster from one-gallon containers, which now reaches more than 50 feet high and looks like a real oasis in a Southern California desert.

THE FREEZE OF 1972

Most of Ruth's plants made it into the newly constructed planting beds during the summer of 1972. That December, a freak cold snap brought snow and freezing weather to the San Francisco Bay Area. The inland valleys, including Walnut Creek, were hid hardest. Ruth's plants may have survived these conditions if they had been further established, but because they were so brand-new to the outdoors and so small they were especially tender, and the vast majority died. When the spell passed, Ruth found limp agaves and drooping yuccas. Always the meticulous record keeper, she documented the extensive damage. Nina, who had just graduated from college, remembers the list of dead plants reaching 40 pages. Only a few made it through the frost. For all intents and purposes, Ruth's collection was gone.

The aftermath of the December 1972 freeze—dead aloes in bed 7. ▲

Very young *Butia capitata* surrounded by snow on the ground from the 1972 freeze. ▲▲

Borrowing Phil's cap (more as a joke than for any meaningful sun protection), Ruth stands in front of her collection of homemade frost covers. ◄

After the 1972 freeze, Ruth replanted, but this time with protective covers over anything she feared to be tender. ▲

At age 64, with the majority of her collection decimated by a freak freeze, laying down her shovel would have been totally understandable. But as soon as conditions were amenable, Ruth started tracking down plants and getting them into the ground. "I figured it doesn't happen that often," she recalled, "and you can't just not replant those same things, because they might have another twenty years before they'd be killed again. So I'm just replanting." Ruth's daughters concurred that their mother was never one to cry over spilled milk. "She'd clean it up," said Nina. "And then go back out and milk the cow," Kathy finished.

In late winter, Ruth and Phil traveled to Southern California with the family station wagon to purchase replacement plants. Although he was never particularly interested in the plants, Phil always supported Ruth. Longtime friend Wayne Roderick remembered, "Phil Bancroft just adored Ruth, and he wanted her to have anything she wanted. After the Big Freeze, when they made three trips to L.A., he went along and did the driving and made certain the plants got well packed into the car. He did everything he could to help her."

Although Ruth kept gardening after the Great Freeze, the experience left a scar. To prevent a repeat occurrence, she designed and built more than 300 custom wooden frames, covered them tautly with plastic, and placed them over tender plants. "It took me weeks to figure out what frame to put on what plant," she said. "And it took two men over a month to do it, five or six weeks." These covers dot the garden from early winter through the last chance of frost in spring and, like the folly, have become instantly recognizable parts of Ruth's garden.

A special little home built for tender *Furcraea*. ◄

If a plant was at risk for damage, Ruth built a cover for it. ►

A collection of plants protected by covers, including *Cereus* cactus with a bag over its head. ◄ ◄

The Climate of Walnut Creek

While Walnut Creek is included in the Bay Area region, it is much hotter in summer and colder in winter than more coastal locations like San Francisco or even Berkeley. During especially cold storms, snow falls on nearby Mount Diablo, but snow on the valley floor is rare. Walnut Creek's warm-summer Mediterranean climate mimics other California interior valleys. Summer is hot and dry, virtually devoid of precipitation. In winter, Pacific storms reach Walnut Creek, bringing rain. The average annual rainfall in non-drought years hovers around 20 inches. The average rainfall has not changed drastically since Ruth first planted her garden (except in a drought year), but every year the rains become more erratic. The first rain used to arrive in October, and it would come steadily through spring. Now the first rain sometimes does not happen until December. As these winter rains are less and less reliable, we need more and more dry gardens.

Ceiba speciosa with its winter covering in the early 1980s. ◄

Surrounded by hardier agaves, *Myrtillocactus geometrizans* sits protected from winter under one of Ruth's signature cold frames. ▶

The covers also help mitigate wet winter soil, another major challenge. Most of the succulent plants in the collection originate in regions with summer rains (albeit sparse) and winter drought. Some of these plants do not like cold, damp soil during the winter—the roots simply rot in those conditions. The plastic covers were Ruth's security blanket while she experimented and pushed the limits on what she could grow.

Ruth covered every vulnerable plant for as long as it would reasonably fit in a cage (although *reasonably* is subject to interpretation). She planted a silk floss tree (*Ceiba speciosa*) in the mid-1970s. It is known for being tender when young, so she put one of her plastic covers over it. The size of the cover increased every year until the tree grew to 12 feet tall. Ruth tried to keep the trunk covered, poking holes in the plastic for the branches. She diligently protected it for years. Ultimately, in the 1980s, it just got too big to cover. In 1990 there was another big freeze when an Alaskan front came down and froze most of the state. The tree lost all of its branches, which blackened and had to be cut off. But that spring, Ruth noticed that the trunk seemed to be living underneath the bark, so she left it in place. Sure enough, it bounced back, more vigorous than ever. Its dazzling pink blooms put on an especially grand show that fall. This tree, a testament to Ruth's patient caretaking, continues to be a showstopper each September and October, at a time of year when few other trees can compete with its performance.

A walk-through frost cover shields bed 6, filled with mostly tender small succulents (and a large plant of variegated *Agave americana*).

Flower stalks on *Erythrina ×bidwillii* grow 2 to 3 feet long, with individual petals measuring 2 inches long. ▲

Erythrina ×bidwillii forms a handsome shrub tipped with bright red flowers from summer into fall. ▶

The freeze also inspired Ruth to keep more doubles of some plants growing in the ground. Plants got a trial run to see if they could survive the conditions; if they perished, Ruth always had extras. Because of this backup system, even with three additional acres of in-the-ground garden space, Ruth never emptied any of the greenhouses (as Phil was hoping might happen).

The freezes did not deter Ruth—they often just fueled her experimentation. The shrub coral tree (*Erythrina ×bidwillii*) near the folly should have grown to resemble a tree. But whenever it nearly reached tree stature, a bad winter knocked it back to the ground. Ruth changed her pruning technique and cut it all the way down to the ground each winter, letting it grow into a bushy shrub topped with bright red flowers each summer. The short form is an unexpectedly beautiful way to show off the tree, as it keeps the flowers at eye level.

Ruth did not garden according to anyone else's rules or in hopes of setting an example. She had no guidebook on how to grow these plants—largely too tender and too sensitive for the extreme highs and lows of Walnut Creek—in her area. She had no one but herself to impress, and she was gardening only to learn. "I'm pushing in the garden, too, things that are not supposed to be hardy here," she said. "I've tried a number of them, and some do all right, and some don't. But I always like to try something, if I like the plant itself. See how it will do."

This experimentation was not restricted to hardiness. Ruth once discovered that *Yucca carnerosana* had a rotten spot in its trunk. Upon carving it out, she discovered that the cavity almost went through the entire trunk of the plant. She shoved a piece of wood into the space to act as a support and hoped the tree would survive.

If you look closely at the trunk, you can see the block of wood supporting *Yucca carnerosana*. Ruth placed it in the empty cavity around a rotten spot, and the plant grows around it.

Ruth feared that even with the wooden support, water would puddle in the cavity in winter, causing further damage. To prevent this, she fastened a metal sheet to cover the wound as a sort of metallic bandage. Eventually the tacks holding the metal fell out and the sheet dropped away, leaving the wooden support exposed. Rather than repair it, the crew decided it was a fascinating learning opportunity (as well as very cool) to see a tree supported by a block of wood. As a testament to Ruth's willingness to experiment, to this day the yucca just keeps on growing and thriving.

Ruth practically lived in the garden. She once said she loved the garden because it gave her a chance to do exactly what she chose to do, without supervision from anyone. She worked seven days a week, morning to night, barely taking breaks. She did not drink enough water and never wore sunscreen (although you would never know it from her porcelain skin). After spending her day in the garden, she recorded everything she did that day. No matter the season, she perused catalogs and made selections. Wayne Roderick called her a true dirt gardener, a perfect description of this small, forceful woman who did everything with her bare hands—she did not even wear gloves!

The bright pink fall bloom of commanding *Ceiba speciosa*.

Ruth gardened slowly and meticulously, and she directed her few hired hands to do the same. Brian calls her an exacting taskmaster, very confident in what she wants and how she wants it done. Martin Viveros, a loyal gardener from 1991 through today, remembers being completely scratched up after his first day on the job. Used to mow-and-blow tasks, he was tempted to flee. But he started watching Ruth, sans gloves, move through the garden gracefully. She had mastered a sort of dance one must learn when working with these dangerous plants—how to reach into a nolina, which has harmless-looking leaves that can slice your skin like it is butter, and not get a scratch. And when she did get pricked, she was unfazed. "If I stopped for every little scratch, I'd get nothing done," she once told Brian. Mostly, she took her time and went slowly. Working with cactus and succulents truly requires patience. In the short term, you must be careful with how you navigate them or you will end up with an arm full of spines. And their slow-growing habits require long-term endurance—a kind of paradigm shift toward slowing down and letting nature take its time.

In the garden, one task held a particularly soft spot in Ruth's heart: she loved to weed. In 1991 she said, "Every time I go out I decide I am going to do a certain thing, and I'm not going to do any weeding, and I end up doing the weeding. Every time. So that was it today, again. I got about a half a bucket." The most common weed on her property was spotted spurge (*Euphorbia maculata*), which happens to be one of her favorite genera. This relative, however, is a persistent weed capable of producing 500 seeds per square feet in just two weeks' time.

This lovely vignette includes the trunk of *Washingtonia filifera*, the large, sword-like leaves of *Doryanthes palmeri*, and volunteer *Dasylirion* between them with *Yucca filifera* in back. *Bulbinella nutans* blooms in bright yellow, contrasting against a blue cycad, and *Aloe distans* offers scrumptious texture in front. ◄

Ruth's garden fills in. *Chamaerops humilis*, *Eucalyptus polyanthemos*, and a Torrey pine offer a canopy for aloes, agaves, and the rest of Ruth's collection. ◄ ◄

OPENING THE DOORS TO THE PUBLIC

Although most of Ruth's neighbors had no clue about her collection, people in horticultural circles near and far were catching wind. A wall between the garden and the street was built when it became public, but for the decades that Ruth tended the garden on her own, there was just a split rail fence separating her from any passersby. Interested parties showed up—often with no advance notice—to find Ruth in the garden. She always made time to talk plants with anyone who showed an interest. The garden became a frequent field trip for plant identification classes at Diablo Valley College, visits from UC Berkeley landscape architecture students, aspiring designers, and obsessive plant collectors. Local designers and horticulturalists knew they could rely on Ruth's garden as a living laboratory of what would grow and succeed in their climate.

Word of Ruth's garden reached Frank Cabot, a well-known alpine rock plant collector with gardens in Cold Spring, New York, and Murray Bay, Quebec. He had always considered dry-adapted cactus and succulents to be hostile and of little interest. But on a visit to California for a conference, he stood in Ruth's garden and knew instantly he was "in the midst of a great garden and in the company of a great gardener." What really impressed him was the layout of plants, which showed off textures, shapes, and colors with grace and artistry that rivaled any garden he had ever seen.

Green-branched *Parkinsonia aculeata*, yet to leaf out, spreads its boughs over a giant blue clump of *Agave americana* (*A. rasconensis*) and a swatch of smaller and greener *Agave mitis* var. *albidior*. *Tanacetum ptarmiciflorum* blooms white in the background, and bright coral blooms of *Gasteria acinacifolia* dangle in from behind the agave.

Manzanita 'Ruth Bancroft', which is a volunteer seedling (it came up on its own), grows on the right, while weeping *Melaleuca preissiana* matches it on the left, creating an archway. *Aloe speciosa* is framed in the archway.

Concerned about the future of his own garden, Frank asked what would happen to Ruth's garden after she lay down her trowel. She did not have an answer. Her children appreciated the dry garden from a collector's point of view, but did not share her interest in maintaining it. On their way home, Frank's wife half-jokingly suggested the idea of a nonprofit organization focused on garden preservation. Land and agricultural trusts exist, so why not one for gardens? Frank mused that Ruth's garden would be the ideal test for such an endeavor. It was so unique, so Western, and so American—it made perfect sense.

Ruth, age 80, and Angela Lansbury at her garden on Founder's Day in 1989 to celebrate the establishment of the Garden Conservancy. Ruth's garden was the first preservation property. ▲

Angela Lansbury acts as honorary chair for the Ruth Bancroft Garden at its inception as a public garden in 1989. ◄

Ruth, age 96, among a clump of *Agave* in 2004. ►

Frank founded the Garden Conservancy in 1989. In 1991, the Garden Conservancy and the Ruth Bancroft Garden began informally raising money for preservation and maintenance. In 1992, the garden opened tours for the public on a limited basis. In 1994, the property was officially transferred to a new nonprofit, the Ruth Bancroft Garden, Inc.

To add some celebrity cachet to the launch, the founding committee of the Garden Conservancy included Angela Lansbury as honorary chair. She toured Ruth's garden in 1989 for the founding of the conservancy. Brian noted that the organization thought it would be a real feather in its cap to have the famous *Murder, She Wrote* star pay a visit. He was tasked with finding a hybrid succulent for Angela to plant in Ruth's garden; his selection was also to be named in her honor. He chose a fantastic gasteria, but the board was not impressed with its lack of flower and asked him to find another. "So I chose a less interesting gasteria but one in flower, and now it's

named *Gasteria* 'Angela Lansbury'. It was a really great affair," Brian said. "Angela was totally delightful. She was prim and proper—not a let-your-hair-down kind of person—but she chatted it up with Ruth and planted the plant."

Public interest in the garden surprised Ruth. "I just started it for the fun of it and the enjoyment of it. I had no idea that people would be looking at it, no idea at all," she said. "I'm sure a lot of people don't care for it. But I'm surprised, really surprised, at the number of people who do like it. That surprises me more." The garden enjoys a reputation world-wide as one of the most interesting collections of cactus and succulents, planted in a climate that is too hot or cold for many of them. Ruth has always remained humble about the impact of her collection. When asked in 1998 about the potential of the garden, Ruth admitted that it could become "an oasis in acres of subdivisions," a place "to relax, breathe more deeply, and enjoy whatever aspect with it that appeals to each individual."

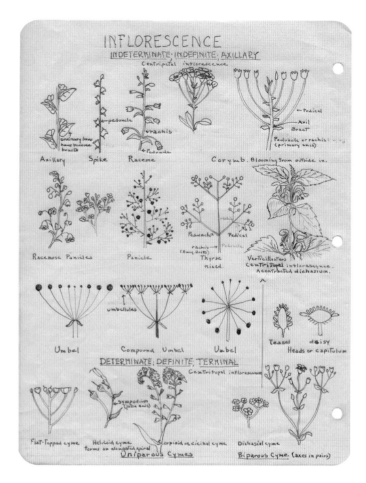

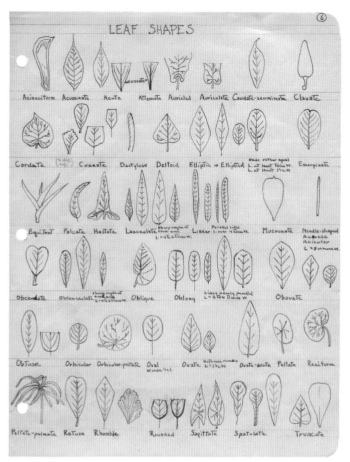

Ruth continued her study of plants away from the garden, including copying illustrations from botanical textbooks. Seen here, different types of inflorescences. ▲

Ruth copied various types of leaf attachment and arrangement. The basal arrangement forms a rosette, a characteristic of so many plants in her collection. ▶

Leaf shapes that Ruth copied. ▼

Ruth, age 100. ▶▶

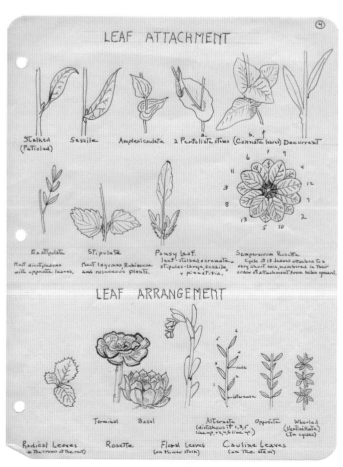

Ruth's children attribute her longevity to drinking two glasses of milk and one of sherry each day. Brian contests that on Wednesdays, the day he worked for many years, gardening was followed by a beer—specifically, Henry Weinhard's Private Reserve ("The sherry was with dinner," he suggested). While bone-building or thirst-quenching hydration might be part of the story, along with fabulous genetics, the garden seems to serve as Ruth's place to immerse herself, likely influencing her ability to stay active. Or maybe it was always her intention to plant glacially slow-growing plants in order to patiently watch them reach maturity. Most likely, her longevity has something to do with her unrelenting quest to keep learning. The garden was a particularly great classroom for Ruth because she never saw it as complete. "Oh, it's never been more than half or three-quarters done to start with," she said in 1991.

One thing is certain: Ruth's insatiable thirst for knowledge only grew. She copied horticultural textbooks by hand to back up her experiential knowledge with academic-level self-taught botany lessons. The more she learned, the more there was to learn. Brian described an infectious enthusiasm when they shared their interests and compiled lists of new plants to track down—lists that grew longer and longer over time.

Ruth was 63 when she planted the garden, and 83 when it opened to the public. She continued working daily well into her nineties. At a doctor's appointment at age 95 she complained of not having as much energy as she used to. When the doctor asked for an example, Ruth replied that after working with a digging fork for three hours in the garden, she had to come in for rest. At 100, Ruth decided she needed to use her walker, and her daily work in the garden came to an end. Her loyal staff adore her, and with the house still a stone's throw from the garden, separated by a fence, they pay weekly visits and keep Ruth in the loop about what is happening outside. Even with declining mobility, Ruth has not stopped learning. She fills her days with reading, opera, classical music, and arranging any seashells into thoughtful miniature compositions, which she likens to small landscape designs.

GARDENING IN THE SPIRIT OF THE FOUNDER

The creed of the Garden
Conservancy is direct: preserve the
garden in the spirit of its founder.

This simple mission proves to be complex, nuanced, and part of an ongoing conversation for everyone who works at Ruth's garden. A living landscape is anything but static. As the test case for the conservancy, the team has had to grapple with how to preserve what amounts to a living piece of art—composed of colors, textures, and forms—that continues to grow and change. Gardening in Ruth's style does not necessarily mean making the exact same planting choices, but rather applying the same principles of passion, experimentation, working in compositions, and a focus on building collections. Having a curatorial team of eclectic, highly focused plant collectors is essential. Three such people—Brian Kemble, Walker Young, and Ryan Penn—found their way to Ruth's garden.

Inside the propagation greenhouse, Brian grows *Aloe, Gasteria, Beaucarnea,* and others from seed. ▲

The propagation greenhouse, where Brian has started seeds and protected tender plants since the 1980s. There is not an inch of plantless space. ◄

Brian started working at the garden in 1980. When he and Ruth met, Brian was vice president of the Oakland chapter of the Cactus and Succulent Society. He had booked Clive Innes from Holly Gate Cactus Nursery in West Sussex, England, as a speaker for the group. When Clive arrived, he mentioned that he wanted to visit an amazing garden in the area. Brian went to see for himself, and he met Ruth. "With a handshake and a beer, I started working for her," he said. Ruth tasked Brian with taking care of plants in the greenhouses before they were planted outside and starting plants from seed. This was a dream come true for Brian, who loves seed propagation, and soon Ruth's collection exploded; the aloe

population alone increased at least tenfold. Phil built a new greenhouse for Brian within the year he started working, and no matter how many layers of shelves were installed, there has never been enough room.

Since the 1980s, Brian has grown the collection, learning the history of every one of the plant acquisitions and their placement in the garden. He was privy to all of Ruth's design compositions, as well as her process for starting seeds and propagating succulents. Brian is the brain trust of the garden's history, and he and Ruth have a unique, mutually admiring relationship. Brian is also a consummate collector. His objects of choice include plants, books, records, art, and stamps.

At right sits Brian's *Aloe humulis* project. He is breeding small South African aloes in search of the bumpiest blue leaves and biggest flower power.

Beyond being the bridge to the garden's past, Brian is a world-renowned succulent expert, particularly in the genera *Agave*, *Aloe*, *Echeveria*, and *Gasteria*. Unlike Ruth, he is not content growing and collecting. He longs to see these otherworldly plants in their native habitats; he feels a spiritual connection when he sees a plant growing in the wild. His plant obsessions have led him to the southwestern United States, Mexico, South Africa, Madagascar, and Namibia (the Canary Islands are his dream). A recent adventure took Brian and Walker to Lesotho to see spiraled *Aloe polyphylla*. Brian timed the trip for late October, when the plants would be in bloom. The morning of his arrival to the mountainous region, he mounted a horse for a two-hour journey through grassland until he reached a dazzling quarter-mile band of spiral aloes in full bloom. After every trip, Brian returns to the gardens with photos to share with Ruth about the origins of her much-loved collection.

Taking the passion even further, Brian is also a breeder, cross-pollinating plants under controlled conditions and growing their offspring from seed. In the greenhouse, he hybridizes aloes in search of longer flower stems on multiple inflorescences, more deeply colored foliage, or more compact growers. In recent years, he is after the bluest and bumpiest *Aloe humilis* hybrid he can create. While she never got into breeding, Ruth was in awe of Brian's talents and wanted him to delve deeply into that world via her greenhouses. A handful of his hybrids are for sale at the on-site plant nursery, and he has introduced a few into the horticultural trade: *Aloe* 'Wunderkind' and *A*. 'Hellskoof Bells' are available in the United States, and *Agave* 'Blue Brian' is for sale in Europe.

A moonlight cactus (*Selenicereus*) climbs up the shade cloth at dusk.

Walker and Ryan are ushering in the newest generation of quirky plant collectors who find their way to the garden. After falling in love with succulents and buying far more than he had room for, Walker attended a talk, led by Brian, on plant oddities at nearby Annie's Annuals. Brian was struck by Walker's knowledge and enthusiasm and convinced him to start volunteering at the garden. The volunteer work turned into a job in which Walker is able to dig into his passions while surrounded by like-minded experts and fellow collectors. Within flora, Walker is deep into cycads. And, like Brian, he is a plant-based traveler, trekking on long journeys just to see plants in their native habitat in order to replicate those natural conditions in the garden. This informed way of planting—nestling plants against rocks if that is how they grow in nature, or using small trees for dappled light—helps plants from dry conditions around the world thrive in gardens. When Walker comes upon new plants, he remembers the saying that seeing a plant in habitat is like meeting an old friend for the very first time.

Ruth used the shade house for rambling, vining, tender plants. Cradled by a wire support, *Aloe sabaea* (one of Brian's friends nicknamed it "Dreadlock"), which is native to Yemen, hangs in the shade house. The inflorescence does not normally droop downward—it broke, but still seems perfectly happy to bloom.

A tiered planting in the shade house is a treasure box of miniature plants.

One of Walker's main contributions is a complete revamp of the shade house, a protected area of the garden. Ruth used the space for anything she feared too tender for the outdoors, including epiphytic cactus, dragon fruit, and many species of *Euphorbia*. After decades of growth, the shade house was filled with gnarled, vining plants that outgrew the space. There was no barrier between path and bed, and some of Ruth's smallest and most tender plants were subject to trampling once the garden went public. Walker reconstructed the planting beds, mounding them up with several feet of rock and shaping them to mimic the miniature rock outcroppings he has seen on botanical treks. Now the shade house serves as a sort of jewel-box garden, home to especially tender, rare, or nostalgic plants chosen because they are small and will not outgrow their space. Walker admitted there is a bit of snobbery involved in what makes the cut. When you step inside, it is a whole world in miniature. There is a wealth of detail, from small *Haworthia* growing as little stacks of leaves, pure silver *Dyckia* resting perfectly on soil, and nearly black *Eriosyce* cactus from Chile. An entire shade house is not necessary to create a jewel-box garden, however; any gardener can do this at home. Choose a few particularly ornate specimens and nestle them together in a container. Use a top dressing of small buff-colored gravel to give it a sense of a finished composition, reminiscent of a desert landscape in miniature.

The refreshed shade house boasts pint-size curious oddities from around the world. Before the revamp, this entire bed held just one overgrown, incredibly thorny specimen of *Euphorbia milii*. Now it has dozens of plants, including *Pachypodium lamerei* var. *fiherense*, which is tall and topped with a burst of green leathery leaves, and blue columnar *Browningia hertlingiana* from Brazil. ▲

Ruth's original use of the shade house. Vining cactus and euphorbia still tangle themselves at the far end, but now that they are elevated with rocks, they are no longer at risk of being trampled. ◄◄

Purple-pink *Graptopetalum amethystinum* with dazzling yellow and red star-shaped flowers. ▲

Eriosyce heinrichiana (*Neochilenia jussieui*), from Chile, is almost black with a trio of pink flowers. ◄

A trio of silver plants cluster in the shade house. At left, a powdery pachyphytum—a gift from Myron Kimnach, former director of The Huntington Gardens—grows between rocks. At right, *Echeveria setosa* var. *deminuta* forms compact, fuzzy blue rosettes. Below, *Dyckia marnier-lapostollei* looks like it is just resting on the rocks. ◄ ◄

Planted in two main beds, the shade house garden features an important distinction in the garden—a division between summer-dry and winter-dry plants. Although all the garden's plants are from dry regions around the world, those from Mediterranean climates—including the Mediterranean Basin, California, western and southern Australia, western South Africa, and central Chile—all grow in winter, watered by winter rains, and prefer to be dry and dormant in summer. Plants from other dry regions in the world—like parts of Australia, much of the Arabian peninsula, northwestern Argentina, and the deserts of Arizona and Mexico—grow in summer, watered by (sometimes scarce) summer rains, and prefer (if not demand) to be dry and dormant in winter. Staff water both beds in the shade garden gently by hand, and at any time of year one half will likely be in growth while the other half waits patiently for its turn. The winter rainfall side is more obvious when it is actively growing because many of the plants are bulbs that lose their leaves completely by summer. The summer rain section is subtler. Most do not lose leaves and go fully dormant; they merely hang out, waiting for their season.

A collection of *Gasteria*, *Haworthia*, *Crassula*, *Gibbaeum*, and *Pachypodium* specimens.

Home gardeners need not be as extreme in their plant placement. While Mediterranean-climate plants have adapted to withstand drought in summer, very few will mind supplemental summer irrigation—provided (and this is absolutely key) that the soil drains well. Plants that prefer to be dry in winter also require well-draining soil to prevent rot. Ruth's garden is filled with plants from different regions in the same beds. They are watered weekly in the summer, twice a week if there is a heat wave.

Tucked in the back of the shade house is a blue cycad, an important vestige of the garden's past. Ruth was always interested in cycads, but they were expensive and not widely available. These rare, ancient plants feel almost prehistoric, like a dinosaur that might pop up around the corner of the garden. They are very limited in their distribution in the world, but are found in Central and South America, Africa, Asia, and Australia. Cycads are historically seen as status symbols, and many rare ones have been dug out of their natural habitat.

When Ruth got her hands on a blue specimen of *Encephalartos horridus*, she planted it in the shade house—a sure sign she thought it was important. Three decades later, the specimen has reached maturity, measuring a 5-foot mound with ready-to-harvest pups growing up the sides. It produced a cone a few years ago, which indicated that it had reached sexual maturity and that it is female. Females are more valuable than males because, if pollinated, you can get viable seed from them. The garden has only one female plant

Encephalartos horridus was Ruth's very first cycad. She kept it safe in the shade house until she knew it would be hardy outdoors.

of that specimen, so the bright orange seeds inside the 16-inch-tall cone were not pollinated. Walker is working to increase the amount of cycads in the garden, and also determining which ones are hardy enough to live outside. There are now several dozen cycads in the garden, including 20 kinds of *Encephalartos*, along with numerous *Cycas*, *Macrozamia*, and *Dioon*—all outdoors.

These nonflowering plants produce cones, making them closer relatives to conifers than to flowering plants such as palms, despite their frond-like leaves. They are also dioecious, meaning plants are either male or female. The almost plastic or leather-like leaflets come in shades of green and blue. While some are spineless, others are as mean as can be—just as Ruth likes them—and draw blood easily. Cycads appreciate the same conditions as many succulents—fairly intolerant of frost, and best performing in well-draining soils—so they are a great choice to mix in with other dry plantings.

The evolution of the garden, as seen in one bed: Ruth loved *Euphorbia myrsinites*, seen here billowing over the rock edge. Walker echoed the color with a cycad at right, and Ryan planted dark purple *Leucadendron* 'Ebony' to pick up the darker shades of the aloes at right. *Acacia willardiana*, at left, is young but promises eventual dappled light along with its handsome exfoliating bark.

Ruth's plantings in the back—various types of *Opuntia*, *Agave* 'Sharkskin', and an assortment of *Echinops*—represent how she often designed with one of everything. In front, mounds of the same type of *Mammillaria geminispina*, nestled among rock outcroppings, represent how the team evolves the garden by adding more repetition and unity to beds. ▲

Leucadendron 'Ebony' has leathery flowers. ◄

Ryan is another lifelong collector. Landscaping jobs taught him that he enjoyed learning as much as digging. His expertise in Ruth's garden is California natives and Australian plants. His plant voyages rarely take him across country, or even state, borders, but he has been to some of the most remote, wild sections of California to discover more about the native plant life. Ryan has done the most research with manzanitas, dudleyas, chaparral flora, and conifers. Humility is a trait he shares with Ruth, as he fancies himself a generalist rather than an expert. He is particularly captivated with Australian Proteaceae, which can be fussy to grow. He loves the challenge, as well as the reward, when a protea establishes itself successfully.

Ruth's garden started out as that of a collector, although she clearly had an innate sense of design and a plant-driven approach. Within her compositions (which usually involved putting many species of the same genus together in order to compare and contrast differences), she tried to plant things to play off one another, either by serving as backdrops or focal points. Now that the garden is public, it serves a greater good. It is a resource for people who want to see the variation in dry plants and the ways in which to use them in design. Visitors can find different styles and approaches to creating a dry garden. Some parts are designed more like a botanical garden, with specimens too large for a home garden on display. Other parts feel wild and slightly unkempt, like you have stumbled on the plants while hiking. Some sections are clear compositions with a focal point and a supportive cast around it. Because the garden began from a collector's perspective, every plant has a history and a reason for being there.

The garden team negotiates how to evolve the garden gently into a more intentionally designed space. This is a collaborative process, albeit with its own flavor of tension. The gardeners make most choices when a bed is revamped after

Sturt's desert pea (*Swainsona formosa*) is the state flower of South Australia.

years of slow compaction and decreased drainage, which can lead to plant failure. Brian insists that they first look at what Ruth was trying to accomplish in that bed. Was she trying to show off her agave collection? Play with shades of silver foliage? They stick with this original intention and plant accordingly, with a few updates that promote a more cohesively designed garden. For Walker and Ryan, that translates to placing plants in a more naturalistic arrangement that mimics how they grow in the wild. They also echo colors across beds, treating the garden as a whole of related parts rather than as miniature compositions.

Ruth's cold frames are a point of contention. Walker remembers his mother in tears after losing her plants in the 1990 freeze, and he appreciates the frost's emotional impact on Ruth. He also understands her desire to protect her collection, but he finds the plastic covers intrusive. He wants to turn the garden into "a four-season affair," choosing only plants that can survive without extra winter protection. Brian

disagrees: he believes a public garden cannot be indulgent with plastic covers, but he does not want to get rid of them altogether. The frames are crucial in enabling experimentation, as they keep young plants protected during their first few cold seasons. With just a touch of winter protection, the range of plants that can be grown in the climate grows significantly. There is also an odd beauty to the landscape dotted with the handmade covers; they have become as iconic to Ruth's garden as her folly. This is an ongoing conversation each winter, which sometimes includes not covering plants that may not be hardy enough to make it. Passionate collectors in their own right, the team wants to keep experimenting and, like Ruth, allow themselves to fail on occasion.

Ruth was fearless in her plant choices. Although she was in tune with climatic conditions, she did not let cold temperatures prevent her from planting something she wanted to try. The garden is full of new risks and attempts to push the limits. The collection continues to expand,

In this design-forward composition, planted by current staff, white-edged *Agave victoriae-reginae* is repeated in several spots. *Agave flexispina* grows larger at the top of the bed, and *A. utahensis* var. *nevadensis*, native to California and Nevada, hides toward the center at the bottom of the bed. *Eriogonum latifolium* provides the perfect soft foil to all those stiff leaves.

particularly plant groups in which Ruth was interested and that hold great potential for a dry garden, including California natives and Australian plants.

Australian plants represent an interesting growth point for the garden. Ruth was interested in them, undoubtedly influenced by Lester Hawkins, who was passionate about Australian plants for dry California gardens. She never fully built out this component of the garden, largely because of the limited availability of plant material. This rugged yet beautiful plant palette is diverse as can be, including everything from shrubs like *Banksia*, *Grevillea*, and *Westringia*, trees like *Acacia* and *Eucalyptus*, and wildflowers as bizarre as Sturt's desert pea (*Swainsona formosa*).

Bay Area gardeners often turn their attention to plants hailing from the southwestern coast of Australia because the climates of the regions are so similar. But there is a major difference: the Australian soil is sandy and acidic, and it has perfect drainage—a far cry from Northern California's clay soil, which must be amended to grow dry-adapted plants successfully. The east coast of Australia, while subject to summer rains and occasional flooding, has heavy clay soil. And while plants from this region are used to summer rainfall, many prove adaptable to winter rains instead. As we learn more about plants from Down Under, and as they become more widely available in the horticultural trade, they open up a new realm of plants with which to experiment in U.S. dry gardens.

The grand entrance as visitors arrive to the garden.

INSPIRING THE NEXT GENERATION

Until the garden became public and a wall was constructed between the garden and Bancroft Road, only a split rail fence separated Ruth's plants from the public. While the vast majority of people drove right by, many interested souls found their way to Ruth. She was always most content working quietly in the garden, but she would drop everything to talk plants with an inquiring mind, and her garden has long served as an inspiration to plant lovers, collectors, and designers. Today, a changing climate gives Ruth's experiment with drought-tolerant plants a whole new relevance. Although she did not begin the garden with any environmental or educational aspirations, her creation is now among the best examples of dry-adapted residential landscapes, and by 1998 she had realized that it might serve as an important community resource. "Having children visit the garden is most valuable," she said. "Some may have never been to a larger garden, and it could affect their futures."

With grants from the water district of Contra Costa County, the plant collection now serves as an educational center for children, homeowners, and gardeners to learn more about incorporating drought-tolerant plants into the landscape. Hundreds of schoolchildren make their way through the garden each year with the purpose of understanding water conservation. Each one squeezes *Sedum ×rubrotinctum* in his or her fingers until a drop of water comes out. Just as those generous neighborhood iris breeders of Berkeley inspired Ruth, the garden is serving the next generation of budding plant enthusiasts. All the children take home a jelly bean sedum, perhaps to grow their very own collection.

Historic *Phoenix canariensis*, which formed the palm allée of the Bancroft estate, frames the store. Visitors can shop at a nursery that includes the garden's own introductions.

Ruth's garden proves that a dry garden can still be colorful and flowery. Here, *Aloe striata* rests on a bed of *Cephalophyllum*. ◄

Under the canopy of *Eucalyptus cephalocarpa*, *Aloe* 'Hercules' (one of the tallest-growing aloes in the world) shows off its smooth stem. Below it blooms *Aloe wickensii*, while *Agave americana* (*A. rasconensis*) brushes up against the tree's bark. ◄ ◄

Volunteer opportunities in the garden range from college internships in development, graphic design, and nursery management to event hosting and art-show coordination. Classes offered on weekends include propagation, succulent crafts, and deep dives into some of Ruth's plant collection.

In addition to managing and growing the collection, the team is also transforming the garden into a full-fledged retail nursery for water-saving plants, including some of Brian's hybrids. It is quite a treat to find world-famous experts on staff at a demonstration garden attached to the nursery. Now anyone inspired by the garden can take a piece of it home, and perhaps grow it into their own collection.

Ruth's bold move of planting dry-adapted plants is shifting from the fringe to the norm, and her garden is an example of how to use these plants in a graceful way. The garden's Lawn to Landscape program continues to draw more demand as people remove their thirsty turf grass and replace it with something much more appropriate to a dry-summer climate.

Education is a natural extension of Ruth's collection, and although still humble, she was on board with opening up her garden if people might learn from it. She planted the garden for the purpose of learning, and she was all too pleased when someone else showed interest. When a professor of horticulture at nearby Diablo Valley College discovered the garden, Ruth encouraged him to bring his students out for regular field trips. Her successors are similarly passionate about sharing the garden. The space proves you can have a stunning landscape, full of color, texture, and seasonal change, without relying on water-loving plants. Local gardeners do not have to imagine what something might look like without ever seeing it in real life. Without intending to do so, Ruth's courage to plant the oddities that struck her fancy has paved the way for more people to switch to these climatically appropriate plants.

SIGNATURE PLANTS OF THE DRY GARDEN

Created by meticulous plant
aficionados and tended with love,

collectors' gardens—typically filled to the brim with one of everything—are notoriously charming and always interesting, but not necessarily the best candidates for design lessons. But the magic and beauty of Ruth's garden is that although it is chock-full of thousands of varieties of plants, it is also designed cohesively to offer a sense of tranquility. Ruth's early dreams of landscape architecture found their full realization in her dry garden. The structural, graphic plants she chose contributed to the garden's success, as did her thoughtful attention to principles such as unity, repetition, and balance. Many of the plants have been in the ground for more than four decades and have reached full maturity, standing tall or growing wide. Their stature helps anchor the space.

In a clear example of repetition, fuzzy columnar *Oreocereus celsianus* stands front and center, with another at far right. Towering, shaggy *Yucca rigida* mimics the verticality of the cactus, while the tops of the yucca match the silver-green spiky leaves of *Dasylirion wheeleri* bumping up against the cactus.

Blue *Agave flexispina* and chalky white *Dudleya brittonii* throw inflorescences upward. *Mangave* 'Macho Mocha' and *Opuntia santa-rita*, while different shapes, have matching green and purple speckled colors, making for a magnificently unified scene.

These plants' adaptations to cope with limited water gave rise to many of their most striking features. They evolved in creative ways to conserve precious moisture in the harshest conditions, in turn producing some of the most unexpected flora and most interesting elements to play with when building a garden.

When examining Ruth's garden, it is helpful to break down the palette into their plant forms in order to understand how it evolved over time. Ruth used small succulents like tiles and combined them to form intricate mosaic-like patterns. Agave and cactus establish bold, structural focal points. Yucca and other sword-like leaved plants dot the landscape as radiating globes. California natives, wildflowers, and other delicate perennials provide a much-needed softer side, while trees offer a canopy layer and add verticality. The takeaways for gardeners are many.

The flower of *Echeveria leucotricha* is notable for its fine white hairs.

In the background, *Trithrinax campestris* grows in a bed of green *Dyckia encholirioides* and silver-blue *Senecio mandraliscae*. In the foreground, the trunk of *Yucca carnerosana* stands tall, while *Yucca* 'Bright Star' shines, surrounded by *Tradescantia* 'Purple Heart' and rosette-shaped *Aeonium* hybrids.

THE SMALLEST PLAYERS

There is so much to look at in Ruth's garden that it is almost overwhelming. An immediate place to grab your attention is at ground level. Small succulents are enchanting, and can serve as puzzle pieces that can be placed together in endless combinations. Many seem like they would be best suited under the sea, and being in a garden with succulents can feel reminiscent of exploring tide pools. The bite-size fleshy leaves, often arranged in rosettes, come in the wildest assortment of colors, from pale lavender to bright orange. They are often the gateway plant to a dry palette, just as *Aeonium* 'Glenn Davidson' was for Ruth so many years ago.

And when their delicate flowers sprout, they get exponentially more fascinating. Plants in Crassulaceae, like *Echeveria*, *Dudleya*, *Cotyledon*, and *Pachyphytum*, boast lovely flower stalks, often with pendulous blossoms requiring a bend at the waist to get the full view. These shallow rooters need little space under soil, so they are perfect to pack together tightly for an instantly grown-in look. The majority stay small, so they work best in the front of dry borders where they can be seen, such as edging up against a hardscape. They are also perfect candidates for container compositions that serve as the finishing touches for a garden or patio.

Ruth's favorite way to plant these succulents was to create arrangements—sometimes large paisley swathes—that showed off the varying colors and forms of these small fleshy-leaved succulents. These tapestries offer bold drama at the ground level, with some aeoniums for added height, making them a great choice for the front of borders, closest to paving or pathways. Most of these small plants appreciate protection from sun and cold, so they also do great in pots that can be moved to a warmer spot, if needed, or a location with dappled shade. When mass planting a large group of low growers, adding slight topography to the bed will give it more visual interest. This technique is shown off in bed 6, which is a large, arching bed with plenty of undulating rocks. The permanent overhang provides dappled light in summer, and when used to support plastic, it becomes a walk-in hoop house in winter.

Ruth saved bed 6, with its permanent shade structure, for small, tender succulents that prefer filtered light to full sun.

Graptoveria 'Fred Ives' is common and easy to grow, and it has a great color range from orange to bronze to lilac. ◄

Small succulents, such as the mix of *Graptopetalum* and *Sedum* seen here, make for satisfying color-blocked plantings. ▲

A study in pink: *Euphorbia fimbriata*, *Aloe vacillans*, and a *Graptoveria* hybrid. ▼

Dark purple *Aeonium* 'Zwartkop', far right, adds height to the planting, while the bright green rosettes of a hybrid aeonium form a mound on the right.

Small succulents need not be quarantined: they play very well with other dry plants, either in the landscape or in containers. Unless you are in a milder winter climate than Walnut Creek or willing to cover plantings every winter, consider frost-tolerance levels before creating large landscapes of small succulents. Great drought-tolerant companion plants that help small succulents pop include fuzzy *Stachys byzantina*, silver-leafed *Pelargonium sidoides*, or clumps of petite *Festuca glauca* 'Elijah Blue'.

AEONIUM

Aeonium 'Glenn Davidson' was the first succulent Ruth owned. It is no wonder that the plant's form appealed to her: whether they grow tall, stay flat, or form mounding bushes, all aeoniums (within Crassulaceae) have fleshy rosette shapes. There are at least 35 species, mostly native to the Canary Islands. Aeoniums are monocarpic but usually grow in a clump of multiple stems; when they flower, you might not even notice any dead plants. Most aeoniums prefer a touch of shade except under cooler coastal conditions. Many people are surprised when the aeonium they purchased as a flat or short-stemmed rosette eventually grows taller and forms elongated stems, sometimes upright and sometimes meandering. In the dry garden, they are allowed to express themselves exactly as they want to, and they often give succulent compositions some height, adding verticality in perfect proportion to lower-growing rosettes. Because their scale is usually a bit larger than the smallest rosettes growing at ground level, aeoniums can also mix in with larger landscaping plants.

Blooming *Aeonium* 'Zwartkop'. ▲

The variegated foliage of *Aeonium* 'Sunburst'. ▼

Beautiful rose-tipped leaves of a hybrid aeonium. ▶

The especially cupped leaves of a hybrid aeonium. ▶ ▶

Aeonium 'Glenn Davidson' is hardly the most remarkable aeonium compared to the rest of Ruth's collection, but Brian nurses it along in the propagation greenhouse, hoping to reproduce the plant and reintroduce it outside without losing it.

The extensive assortment in Ruth's collection includes fuzzy-stemmed *Aeonium smithii*; *Aeonium simsii*, which causes a stir each spring when it bursts into flower; *Aeonium nobile*; and *Aeonium castello-paivae*, an echeveria lookalike.

Stacked *Crassula columella* just beginning to flower at the tips.

CRASSULA

Crassula species, among the most bulletproof of these small succulents, hail from South Africa. Some form clumps, like sedums, while others grow into stacked stems and form juicy tails. Ruth has many types in her collection, although the intense geometry of the stacked forms was clearly her favorite. Some of the best examples of stacked plants in the garden include *Crassula columella*. Red *C. atropurpurea* is a notable paddle-leaved variety. Crassula plants work best in miniature compositions in containers, where their geometry is more likely to be noticed and appreciated. In the landscape, choose larger varieties, including fairy crassula (*C. multicava*), which makes a durable ground cover topped with loose clusters of pink-and-white flowers. Silver jade (*C. arborescens*) is a more interesting version of a jade plant, with oval blue leaves that look handsome among other blues, including *Festuca glauca* 'Elijah Blue'.

Blood-red *Crassula atropurpurea*.

Echeveria 'Hummel #2' and a dyckia make a lovely contrast of soft and spiny.

A cluster of *Echeveria agavoides*. ▲

An outcropping of a blush-colored, cold-tolerant *Echeveria* hybrid (*E. agavoides* × *E. colorata*) has neat, symmetrical waxy leaves. ▼

A different metabolism

In order to conserve moisture in harsh conditions, many succulents have a different metabolism than most plants, which breathe through stomata (pores) that open during the day. Succulents have a reduced number of stomata on their leaves, and these open only at night. This phenomenon, known as Crassulacean Acid Metabolism (CAM), allows them to save water during the hottest part of the day and open themselves up to transpiration during cooler nighttime hours.

ECHEVERIA

Echeveria plants—mostly from Mexico—are the darlings of the small succulents. They are always rosette forms and might be fuzzy or lumpy, or have frilly tips, a powdery coating, or a metallic sheen. They come in a range of colors, from palest pink to the deepest purple. Ruth loved *Echeveria agavoides*, whose painted leaves resemble a miniature agave. Walker is another fan of this plant and uses it liberally, often as a filler or ground cover, as the garden becomes a more design-forward space. Echeverias form an arching stalk of long-lasting bell-shaped flowers. Mexican *Graptopetalum*, another staple in Ruth's collection, looks like an echeveria growing on longer cascading stems.

Pachyphytum, also from Mexico, resembles a plump echeveria with balloons for leaves. Hens and chicks (*Echeveria* ×*imbricata*) is one of the most vigorous and reliable choices for larger-scale ground cover plantings.

HAWORTHIA

Haworthia is a curious group of plants from South Africa. Some forms, like *H. cymbiformis*, blend in with other small succulent rosettes and do not particularly stand out. Other varieties, however, are among the most fascinating succulents, and Ruth collected many of these. Zebra-like *H. attenuata* boasts striped bands on its leaves. Some have window-like translucent foliage. Some of the most sought-after forms grow flat-topped, fleshy leaves, like those of *H. truncata*. Others are textured or patterned, such as the pearls on *H. pumila* or the bars on *H. limifolia* var. *striata*. Because many *Haworthia* are small and green, and thus get lost in a larger landscape, Ruth kept a great deal in her greenhouses. A lot of them now live in the protected shade house, where their jewel-like qualities are on full display. Like the other small rosettes, haworthias are a great choice to mix and match with other pint-sized jewels for miniature landscapes in containers.

Lovely webbed tips of *Haworthia arachnoidea*. ▲

A collection of small haworthias. ▶ ▶

Sedum dasyphyllum, aptly nicknamed blue carpet.

SEDUM

Sedum is a diverse genus native to the Northern Hemisphere, especially concentrated in Europe and Mexico. The group is heterogeneous, so much so that plants are being shuffled into different genera. Certain northern types with larger leaves are now classified as *Hylotelephium* (one famed example is *H.* 'Autumn Joy'). These varieties are noteworthy for their extreme hardiness and are a great choice to use in dry gardens in colder regions. Many are low-growing ground covers, perfect for using in rock gardens, over walls, or as low-growers in borders. They also work well in containers, where they fill spaces between small, structural rosettes and often dangle over the sides of planters.

A lovely composition of pink-tipped *Graptosedum* 'Poindexter' at top, surrounded by a few stems of blue *Sedum rupestre*. Green, tiny-leafed *Sedum acre* makes up the largest clump, while an unknown sempervivum hybrid echoes the rosette shape at the bottom. ▶

Dazzling miniature blue leaves of *Sedum rupestre*. ▲

SEMPERVIVUM

Sempervivum, native to Central and Southern Europe, is another small succulent rosette. This genus is monocarpic, meaning plants flower only once before dying. Before their demise, they produce offsets (known as pups or chicks) at their base, which form a ring around the mother plant. Sempervivums are so effective at making a patch of plants that dead mother plants are usually not even noticeable in a clump.

Sempervivum arachnoideum appears to be covered in cobwebs.

A hybrid sedum, *Echeveria agavoides*, and blooming *Haworthia turgida* nestle among boulders and smaller rock mulch.

THE IMPORTANCE OF ROCK

Rocks, from boulders to small gravel, belong in a dry garden. From a soil-health standpoint, they are crucial for mitigating heavy clay soil and increasing drainage. Many dry plants love growing among rocks, as they originate from sheer cliffs, loose screes, or inorganic gravelly soil. But rocks also have an aesthetic appeal. Dry plants can be planted closely together for a lush look, but so many have strong structural appeal that it makes sense to give them space in which they can be appreciated. We all know the look of a landscape with a few cactus and way too much gravel: it is parched and unnatural, like a mail-ordered xeric landscape that was plopped down as soon as the turf came out. Dry gardens can be much more dynamic than this. It is crucial to use a substantial amount of plants of different forms, sizes, and textures, but rocks also have a crucial role. A neutral buff color blends the plant material into more wild regions without calling too much attention to itself. Skillfully bury boulders to expose only the top third or so, which gives the appearance that they are rooted in place. Rocks add year-round structure as plants go in and out of the growing and flowering seasons, adding a visual weight and anchoring effect to any garden. Walker believes that planting the rocks is as important as planting the plants.

Different sizes of rocks form an undulating, naturalistic planting bed.

At the time of the garden's construction, Ruth was not thrilled with Lester's original installation of easy-to-source moss rock. She thought warmer hues would match the surroundings better. In 1975, she was able to strike a deal with a quarry several miles away at the base of Mount Diablo for a one-time giant purchase of rock. The stones were emptied in big piles around the garden, and it took Ruth several months—and hired help—to finish placing the rocks into planting mounds. The beautiful travertine rock came in banded shades of browns and purple-grays, the perfect hues to make the dry-adapted silver-blue and green plants pop. Ever the brilliant designer, Ruth opted to use the same stone everywhere in the garden. The smallest pieces remained on the paths, larger boulders were placed in the beds, and medium-size rocks served as mulch between the plantings. Represented in different sizes, the rock unified the entire garden. But Ruth never had enough. The quarry closed before Ruth could purchase more rocks, and struggled to secure a steady supply.

Sourcing great rock continues to be a challenge, as the selection of rocks sold in landscape yards is usually too homogenous. The garden now sources its rocks from a quarry on Mount Diablo. This scrape-away rock has no commercial value, as it is removed to get to the valuable rock beneath. The garden staff convinced the quarry to save it and sell it to the garden. Once the rock is in his possession, Walker hand sifts it, dividing it into piles of different sizes to keep the larger ones on hand as he builds mounds.

Creating miniature rock outcroppings is a skill requiring patience and practice. Walker starts at the top of a mound and traces about 10 percent down, where erosion would make the boulders pop out. He places flat parts against the side of the mound, mimicking the way water would have shaped the rock. The last touch is a layer of rocks as top dressing, like mulching as an art form. Walker places coarser material at the top of mounds, hiding behind rocks, where bigger chunks might have gotten caught. Finer, more alluvial pieces fall forward, cascading to the bottom of the mound. As soon as he is done, he blasts it all with a hose to make erosion occur naturally.

Any rock will do, but Walker always tries to get his hands on the biggest he can—even twice as big as what he thinks will fit—because he knows that rocks settle drastically over time. Historical photos of the garden show the rocks looking much more prominent. Part of that is sinking, but plants also grow in and swallow head-size rocks in a year or two. If you cannot find big rocks, try fitting together smaller rocks to look like a larger one that has shorn apart or fractured. Once the rocks are in place, it is planting time.

Echeveria derenbergii, at left, and hybrid *E. amoena*, at right, find their homes among jagged rocks.

Ruth's garden is full of stunning architecture. Here, columnar *Oreocereus celsianus* and *Cleistocactus* shoot upward from mounding *Deuterocohnia*, a terrestrial bromeliad. *Yucca treculeana* adds a dramatic backdrop.

ARCHITECTURAL ELEMENTS

Ruth's garden is almost an embarrassment of riches when it comes to dramatic, sculptural elements. These dry plants offer graphic, year-round structure, and many are the most recognizable desert shapes. In a dry garden, the majority of these structural elements are rosette shapes—larger versions of her small tiled plants—or round in nature, both of which make fantastic focal points throughout the garden that are visible from far away. The garden also uses cactus in all forms—paddles, rods, columns, and mounds—as living statues. Plants with sword-like leaves create striking silhouettes.

A clump of *Agave franzosinii* forms a massive wall opposite blooming *Senna artemisioides*.

AGAVE

Agaves are the ultimate crowd pleasers. While some varieties stay small (white-edged *Agave victoriae-reginae*; *A. parryi* var. *truncata*, which resembles an artichoke; and wide-leaved *A. colorata* are particularly well suited to smaller home gardens), many grow larger and demand attention as a focal point. They have the hypnotizing appeal of a rosette-shaped succulent and the do-not-get-too-close challenge of terminal or marginal spines, some sharp enough to cause serious injury. Ruth never liked to admit to choosing favorites, but the sheer volume of agaves reveals her love for the plant. It makes sense: Ruth loves plants with personality, and there is no plant group more robust and dramatic than agaves.

Three of the colors in *Agave lophantha* 'Quadricolor' are easy enough to spot: yellow, dark green, and light green. Pink streaks appear in colder winter temperatures. ◄

Especially captivating bud prints on *Agave parrasana*. Brian has taken three separate trips to North–Central Mexico to see *A. parrasana* in habitat: he failed on the first two tries but was successful on the third attempt. ►

There are about 200 recognized species of *Agave*, natively entirely to the Americas, with most originating in Mexico and the southwestern U.S. They were unknown in Europe before Columbus, but once introduced they became a status symbol. Agaves boast a tremendous amount of diversity in leaf size, shape, color, thickness, and spines. Some plants, like Ruth's favorite *A. franzosinii*, grow up to 13 feet in diameter, while other varieties grow no larger than a head of lettuce. While there are spineless species (such as tender *A. attenuata*), most are rosettes of rigid leaves lined with marginal teeth and a dagger-like spine at the tip. Agaves form leaves from a center cone in which they wrap around each other, unfurling from the outside in. While they are still malleable and pressed together, the marginal teeth of one layer make impressions on the layer around it. Known as bud prints, these markings last for the leaf's life span and make compelling patterns in a dry garden.

You can employ agave plants liberally in a dry garden. In areas without frost, use *Agave attenuata*, which stays modest in size and has no sharp edges. It is stunning in a mass planting along a driveway and as a one-off in container arrangements. An agave can stand alone as a structural focal point—tulip-shaped *A. weberi* is an especially sophisticated form—or it can mix well with other plants. For a formal look, combine several with globe-shaped plants, like *Pittosporum tenuifolium* 'Golf Ball' and *P. tobira* 'Cream de Mint', for a modern, formal appearance. Or embrace the desert look and nestle a few among boulders of equal size, with a columnar cactus adding height to the vignette. Just a few plants can achieve an iconic desert aesthetic.

Spectacular rainbow-colored marginal spines on *Agave shawii*. ▲
Agave franzosinii sports an animal print pattern on each leaf. ►

Many agaves are coated with a waxy bloom that helps reflect sunlight and conserve water. This is especially notable on *Agave franzosinii*, which, for unknown reasons, has remarkable patterns where the wax rubs off as the leaves grow. Brian calls this the "lost wax effect," and has not seen it this pronounced on any other specimen in any other garden.

Although it was labeled as *Agave rasconensis* (a synonym of *A. americana*), this clump clearly bears some resemblance to *A. franzosinii*.

In Ruth's garden, many large species of *Agave* serve as bold focal points. Their distinctive architectural structures—often giant fleshy-leaved rosettes—stand out among the surrounding plants. Ruth's collection boasts dozens of species. If you dare to plant one of these in your home garden, make sure you have ample space for it to grow slowly up to 10 feet tall and wide.

Agave salmiana, nicknamed Rumpelstiltskin. ▲

Spherical clumps of blue *Nolina nelsonii* provide a backdrop for columnar *Echinopsis pachanoi*. At its side is green *Agave geminiflora*, which mimics the shape of the nolina, while variegated *Agave americana* 'Mediopicta Alba' pops in front. ►

Ruth has many varieties of *Agave salmiana* in her collection, but one, from the San Diego Botanic Garden, has a curious habit of crinkling at the tips. As the baby grew, the leaves were totally smooth, and Ruth and Brian wondered if the crinkles would ever develop. It took nearly a decade, but now the dimples are in full effect. Brian's pet name for this plant is Rumpelstiltskin.

A total crowd pleaser, *Agave parryi* var. *truncata* is the densest artichoke-resembling agave.

Dark purple spines on the sides of leaves of *Agave parryi* var. *truncata* shine pink in sunlight.

Repetition of the rosette

Ruth's collection, while vast and deep, has a rare type of unity, and it all comes down to the repetition of the rosette. This radial arrangement of leaves around a stem is repeated in her garden in every size, from small to giant. The globes and spirals of leaves dot every unique composition, giving the eye a place to rest in each bed. There are giant rosettes, like the long, meaty leaves of a large agave or aloe. Many of the small succulents are shaped in rosettes, from a ruffled hybrid echeveria to a powder-covered dudleya. The more fibrous-leaved dry plants also make rosettes in every size. Dyckias, whether deep maroon or bright silver-gray, have rigid leaves lined with spines. The leaves of each yucca, dasylirion, and nolina are densely arranged radially around their stem bases. When the plants are backlit, the sun's rays make them look like glowing orbs. Even many of the plants that are not necessarily organized around a rosette display a rounded symmetry, including columnar, barrel, and mounded cactus. The result is that, despite being planted in a wild way, the inherent symmetry of each of these plants makes the garden feel unified and relaxing.

As you design, echo rosettes in multiple parts of the garden, and at varying heights, from sempervivum ground covers to yuccas, with plenty of radial symmetry in between. As you look down a border or at a composition of the yard, your eye will inevitably land on the rosettes.

Rosettes, repeated. Strappy blue leaves of *Agave franzosinii* stand tall in the back left corner, matched in color with blue *Yucca baccata* just in front of it. Below that, needle-leafed *Agave striata* forms orbs with purple halos all along the middle tier. In front, *Agave parryi* var. *truncata* resembles artichokes, while large green *Agave salmiana* var. *crassispina* anchors the right side of the composition.

Death is a slow process with a great show. This *Agave franzsonii* stalk stands more than 30 feet tall for 18 months before it comes down. ▶

Two agaves in flower: *Agave franzosinii* (left) and *A. salmiana* var. *crassispina* (right). ▶▶

Every agave is monocarpic. Brian notes that it is bitter-sweet when one starts to flower because although you are in for a big treat, you are also losing the plant. In the wild, flowering may occur anywhere from 10 to 40 years, depending on the variety. Ruth found that many species flower in fewer years when watered regularly and nourished in her garden. When they bloom, a head produces a flowering stalk with hundreds of small blossoms on one tall spike or a branched panicle. The stalk shoots out of the head with such amazing pent-up energy that it looks like a rocket propelling into space. Flower stalks up to 30 feet tall persist long after the bloom is finished, adding dramatic visual interest to the garden. At some point the dead plant must be removed, and this is no easy task. It usually takes considerable effort to clear the space the dead mother leaves behind. Most varieties produce offsets before blooming, leaving the babies (which are sometimes quite large) to fill in.

An agave plant begins growing the flower stalk that will kill it. ▲

Agave franzosinii produces a tall branching flower stalk. ◄

Agave franzosinii spent all its energy producing its flower. Now the fleshy plant will slowly wrinkle and die. ◄ ◄

Ruth loved the strange rib structure of Mexican *Thelocactus rinconensis.* ▲

A paddle of *Opuntia robusta* flattens under the weight of raindrops. ►

Paddles of an unknown opuntia stand as background for a rod-shaped cholla and blue-green *Agave havardiana.* ► ►

CACTUS

At first, Ruth's collection began with fleshy-leaved succulents. As she planted her dry garden, people brought her plants. And because Ruth's curiosity is easily piqued, the new plant group would intrigue her, and her collection would continue to grow. While cactus were not her initial focus, their iconic forms became an integral part of the dry garden's structure and a huge aspect of the overall collection.

While odd-looking, Peruvian *Cereus* 'Monstrosus' is remarkably easy to grow and highly resistant to rot—perhaps the reason it survived so long and grew so tall in Ruth's garden. ▲

Red razor-sharp spines of *Ferocactus pilosus*. ◄

Paper-like spines of *Tephrocactus articulatus*, a southern Argentinian cactus. Although the species is hardy, it needs perfect drainage to avoid rotting in winter rain. ►

The spines on *Austrocylindropuntia subulata* absolutely glow.

Almost every cactus has spines. Serving to protect against sunburn and predation, spines add a textural element to a dry garden. They lend particular drama at dusk or dawn, when low sunlight backlights them and creates a glowing aura around each plant. After a rainstorm, spines often change colors—dull red becomes ruby red; dusty pink suddenly glows.

As if offering a mea culpa for those deadly spines, cactus have some of the most delicate, tissue paper–like flowers.

Each spring the garden experiences a progressive parade of unfolding blooms, many lasting for just a few days. The barrels bloom in a circle, like a crown. Upright *Cereus* cactus have large trumpet-shaped flowers protruding from their tops and sides that last only a few days at most. Paddled opuntias look like they have flowers tucked behind their ears. Dragon fruit cactus boast enormous white nocturnal blooms, but visitors who arrive after 8 a.m. will miss them.

Pint-sized *Ferocactus cylindraceus* (which will eventually reach up to 6 feet tall) boasts long pink-hued spines that pop in front of *Agave bovicornuta*. ▶

Orange and pink bicolored blooms on a fuzzy hybrid of *Echinopsis formosa*. ▲

The contrast of sharp spines and pale violet flowers is stunning on *Stenocactus ochoterenanus*. ▶

An unfolding spiral of yellow blooms atop *Ferocactus histrix*. ▲

Shaggy *Opuntia polyacantha* var. *erinacea* is native to the American west and cold hardy, and it offers a terrific hot pink blossom. ▶

Oreocereus doezianus, with its bright coral flower standing at attention on the tip. ▲

Pale mauve blossoms stand out against the fuzz of *Oreocereus pseudofossulatus*. ◄

The new growth on *Opuntia robusta* starts off spineless, with a metallic sheen. ▲

The many delicious colors of *Opuntia santa-rita*. ►

PADDLES AND RODS

Brian describes the form of an opuntia as a bunch of Mickey Mouse ears piled up to make a plant. Each plant grows as haphazard jointed pads, usually covered with spines. Native to North and South America, they grow naturally in every part of the United States except northern New England, Alaska, and Hawaii.

While species of *Opuntia* have a bad reputation because of their tiny glochids (small barbed spines that can cause irritation if touched), this fierce personality might be one of the reasons they were among Ruth's favorites. In a landscape, they provide two seasons of color: orange, red, purple, and yellow flowers in spring and the same hues in fruit come fall. Ruth's garden has an annual fruit-tasting tour each October, and *Opuntia robusta* is a consistent favorite. Ruth used large opuntias as dramatic backdrops, while smaller species mix nicely with softer plants, as *Opuntia polycantha* var. *erinacea* does in the California natives bed.

This opuntia has unknown parentage, yet boasts the best-tasting fruit in the garden.

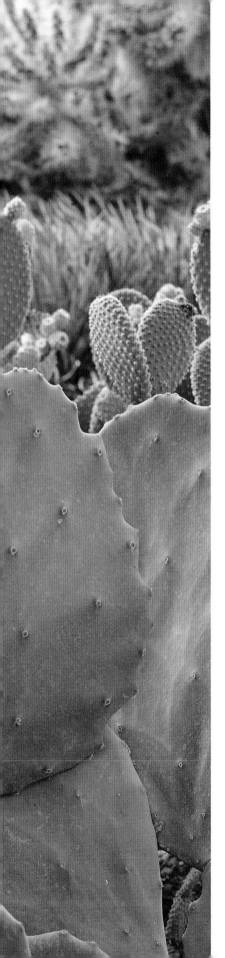

Cylindropuntia rosea spines glow at evening in the garden. ◄

Three different species of *Opuntia* planted together. ◄ ◄

Opuntias showcase the garden staff's tendency to plant multiple species of one genus close to one another to allow for comparison. This is testament to Ruth planting the garden with the mind-set of collector rather than designer. In one of the oldest, most established parts of the dry garden, Ruth clustered different species of *Opuntia*. From one spot, she could observe blue *O. robusta* with fat pads, *O. microdasys* with small polka-dotted glochid clusters, and *O. gomei* 'Old Mexico', a spineless type with undulating paddle edges.

In a home garden, opuntias provide great security systems. Use several at the base of a fence or under a window to deter unwanted visitors. Larger species can screen an unsightly fence while creating a backdrop for smaller dry plants to grow in front. Modest-size types, like *Opuntia santa-rita*, eventually reach 4 feet tall and 6 feet wide, forming a handsome mound of great purple and green pads with bright yellow flowers. Mix an opuntia in with desert penstemon for a blooming desert border. Smaller opuntias,

especially pint-size *O. microdasys*, are adorably statuesque in small geometric pots. Get a few of the same pot, and plant each one with a single *O. microdasys*. Put them on display in a line on an outdoor shelf and enjoy their forms as a piece of living art, but be careful—these are known for having the worst glochids.

Squeeze pads into cylindrical rods and you have another of Ruth's favorites, *Cylindropuntia*. These are the nastiest of all cactus, armed with barbed spines that can detach with just the smallest brush. These fierce defenses likely endeared them even more to Ruth (although she wisely placed them in the middle of beds, out of her way). The silver lining to those dangerous spines is that they glow in backlight. If you are brave enough to plant one in your home garden, try *C. whipplei* 'Snow Leopard'. It is more compact than most, making it more suitable for a smaller space. Spines are white and appear to glow when they catch the light. They are also treacherous, so handle the plant carefully.

COLUMNAR AND TREELIKE

Tall and upright columnar cactus steal the scene in any planting. Native to the Americas, this iconic group includes saguaros (*Carnegiea*), Mexican fenceposts (*Pachycereus marginatus*), and *Cereus hildmannianus*, the first cactus Ruth planted in the ground right outside her garage. Some species sprout arms only after decades of growth. Others grow multiple stems from one base. For all their hefty stature, columnar cactus produce some of the most fleeting and exquisite flowers in the cactus world.

In a part of the garden known as yucca flat, a combination of spiny echinopsis and echinocereus mixes with lumpy *Lophocereus schottii*. ▲

Cereus hildmannianus, the first cactus Ruth planted in the ground. ▶

Mustard-colored unnamed *Cleistocactus* stands tall in the foreground. It pops against a backdrop of *Opuntia robusta*, while *Cylindropuntia rosea* shows off its spines at left.

Columnar cactus are extremely useful in the garden. One approach is to dot them sparingly into compositions as focal points of narrow verticality. Ruth frequently included a few of these at different heights, echoing the straight, narrow form throughout a bed. As with other plant groups, she also amassed plant columns together as a way to explore their similarities and differences. These plants do a great job of screening an unsightly fence. Stick to just one variety for a sleek, modern look, or put many different types together for a more rustic desert effect. They also grow fabulously in planters. A line in a low, rectangular planting makes for easy space dividers in outdoor rooms or on a patio.

Columnar cactus make a screened walkway, with *Yucca treculeana* in the distance. ◀

A collection of South American columnar cactus grows together along the fence dividing Ruth's private home from the public garden. The especially wool-covered ones on the right and in the middle are *Espostoa*. Mounds of *Mammillaria* occupy the foreground. ▼

Over time, columns can become walls in a garden. One such planting is in the area along the fence between Ruth's home and the shade house, where a mix of South American columnar cactus, including *Cleistocactus* and *Espostoa*, grows in close proximity. Where these plantings are more established, the columns stand more than 18 feet tall on either side of a path, forming a walkway hedged with spined and ribbed posts.

Parodia magnifica, organized into neat rows of bristly spines topped with satiny flowers, creates a formal appearance.

SMALL AND ROUND

The garden displays a dazzling amount of small, low-growing cactus from genera including *Mammillaria*, *Thelocactus*, and *Echinocereus*. None is repeated as prominently as *Mammillaria geminispina*. Native to Mexico, this mounding cactus reaches just 8 inches tall, with two types of white spines—long central ones and shorter radial ones—that make each globe look ghostly and glowing. This species is a great choice to add more unity to the landscape, as the silver-white from the spines is echoed in so many of the other plants in the collection, from palm leaves to the waxy bloom on agaves. If you choose a small variety for your own garden, use it liberally.

Mammillaria of unknown species; this is one of the trickier genera to identify. ▲

Although these *Mammillaria* plants look similar, they are not identical species. Slight differences in genera fascinate Ruth. In front, 30-year-old *Mammillaria haageana* (formerly *M. dealbata*) shows its age, forming folds and losing its perfectly cylindrical form. Behind it, an unknown mammillaria sports a perfectly round crown of pink flowers. ◄

Golden barrels (*Echinocactus grusonii*) stand tall with green flesh covered in yellow spines. ◄

Ferocactus pilosus, planted by Ruth, has two types of spines, one thick and one resembling hair, plus a ring of cuplike orange flowers. ► ►

BARRELS

Echinocactus and *Ferocactus*—both barrel genera—have a strong presence in the garden. While scattered throughout, the largest patch of golden barrels (*Echinocactus grusonii*) has been in the same spot since the late 1980s. Before then, Ruth kept losing the plants to rot, so she experimented with different techniques, such as digging them up and tilting them slightly to avoid water accumulation in their center indentations or covering them with plastic to keep out the rain. As with most of her challenges, however, drainage was the real culprit. Eventually the staff learned that barrels do best if planted on a bed of pumice, which provides perfect drainage.

A variety of mounding *Mammillaria geminispina*, upright *Trichocereus*, globe-shaped *Lobivia formosa*, and giant golden barrels share a bed.

In the garden, Ruth largely combined patches of barrels and friends (such as smaller mounding cactus) to once again compare and contrast. As they have matured, the masses of globular form result in playful (yet spiny!) repetition in many of the beds. Barrels leave a strong impression in a home landscape, so show them off in clusters or in a planted pattern. Plant them at the base of taller *Cereus* cactus for a garden of pure architecture. Or sow wildflower seeds between them to give them a season of softness each spring.

A forest of swords capped on either side with silver *Yucca rigida*, tall *Y. rostrata*, multi-trunked *Y. carnerosana*, shaggier *Dasylirion longissimum*, and single-trunked *Y. carnerosana*.

YUCCA AND OTHER SWORDS

A large component of Ruth's garden consists of sword-like globe leaves radiating from a central trunk or stem, including the genera *Yucca*, *Dasylirion*, *Nolina*, and *Beaucarnea*. These bulletproof plants from North America handle heat, aridity, and cold, making them a perfect textural addition to the collection. While they are structural and often rigid, their leaves are usually delicate enough to move in the wind. Sometimes they stay at ground level, like orbs resting on the soil, while others grow tall, adding narrow verticality.

YUCCA

Like cactus, all yuccas are native to the Americas, namely the southern United States and Central America. These are some of the hardiest plants in Ruth's collection. Their leaves are stiff and fibrous, usually tipped with incredibly sharp spikes. Some stay at ground level, like clumps of rigid grass, while others eventually sit atop tall trunks, forming striking silhouettes. They are the ultimate accent plant in a dry garden. *Yucca baccata* is great as a low-growing accent and has a particularly picturesque growth habit. *Yucca carnerosana*, with stiff green swords, is one of the most dramatic varieties, great for marking an entrance or emphasizing a part of the garden. It plays nicely with desert plants as well as more tropical-looking ones. *Yucca rigida* has a softer blue color that makes for a choice silhouette. Gorgeous *Hesperoyucca whipplei* stays trunkless, forming a tight rosette of

A dwarf variety from Utah, *Yucca harrimaniae* has fibers concentrated into an orb shape within its leaves. ▲

Yucca rostrata, a glowing ball of silver-blue, sits surrounded by a blooming *Aloe* hybrid (*A. ferox* × *A. arborescens*). ▶

slender gray-green leaves that come to needle-like points. Most are sharp, so be sure to plant them along walls or in the middle of beds—you do not want to brush against them. Many trunking varieties retain their dead leaves. Some people remove them for a manicured look, but they are left intact in the dry garden to become part of the structural appeal. Ruth preferred the trees to look natural and express themselves as they would in the wild.

In addition to their dramatic trunks and leaves, yuccas bloom with a generous display of white bell-shaped flowers (although not every yucca flowers every year). All yuccas have a symbiotic relationship with a type of moth that pollinates the blossoms at night. When a yucca is planted outside the moth's habitat, the plant will grow, thrive, and flower, but it will seldom produce fruit.

Yucca carnerosana shows off its glorious white blooms, while columnar *Oreocereus celsianus* reaches to match it.

The pendulous bloom of *Yucca filifera*. ▲

Beyond the planting islands, *Yucca rigida*, Ruth's original planting, shows off its shaggy trunks, blue dagger-like leaves, and creamy off-white flowers. To the right, *Yucca treculeana*, of darker green leaf color, also blooms. ▶

Yucca rigida was part of Ruth's original planting, and it has grown into a giant old specimen. It is a prime example of Ruth's preference for letting plants be natural instead of groomed. Brian refers to this as "grass skirt yucca."

Ruth always wanted to grow a Joshua tree (*Yucca brevifolia*), but never succeeded in keeping one alive. Brian had a friend in Healdsburg who moved away in 2013 and left a Joshua tree behind. Along with Ryan, Walker, and Troy, he dug up the 10-foot-tall tree—a much larger size than Ruth normally starts with—and moved it to Ruth's garden, where it is still alive, although as of this writing it has not yet flowered.

Three mature *Yucca* species with dried leaves stand tall in the bed known as east yucca flat. From left to right: *Y. rigida*, *Y. thompsoniana*, and *Y. carnerosana*. A similarly shaped spiny ball of *Agave striata* picks up the same form at ground level. ▲

Ruth's Joshua tree (*Yucca brevifolia*). ◀

OTHER SWORDS

Plants from *Dasylirion*, *Beaucarnea*, *Nolina*, and *Xanthorrhoea* are additional accents whose sword-like leaves are arranged in radiating circles from a central stem. Some are more rigid and radiating, while others resemble verdant fountains and add a tropical feel to a dry garden. The garden uses the plants as backdrops for smaller foreground plantings such as aloes or small agaves. Dasylirions, beaucarneas, and nolinas all have strong, fountain-like silhouettes and make excellent accents alongside a dry palette. The most unsung of this group is *Xanthorrhoea*. These plants, also known as grass trees, have bright green narrow, grasslike leaves that radiate from the top of a thick, slow-growing stem. They are as dry in water needs as yuccas, but the shade of green provides a much lusher look.

The long, needle-like leaves of two *Dasylirion longissimum* specimens make a stunning backdrop for a clump of *Puya coerulea* var. *monteroana*. Evening backlight shines through them in a total celebration of shape, texture, and light. ▲

Australian *Xanthorrhoea* shows off tall brown-topped stalks in the foreground, while *Yucca rostrata* almost perfectly echoes the blue orb shape behind it. At left an *Aloe* hybrid (*A. ferox* × *A. arborescens*) has deeper hued leaves and bright orange-red flowers. ◄

Nolina interrata, the only nolina on the endangered species list, is notable for its woody underground stems. ►

Xanthorrhoea makes a lush green fountain of a backdrop for blooming aloe plants.

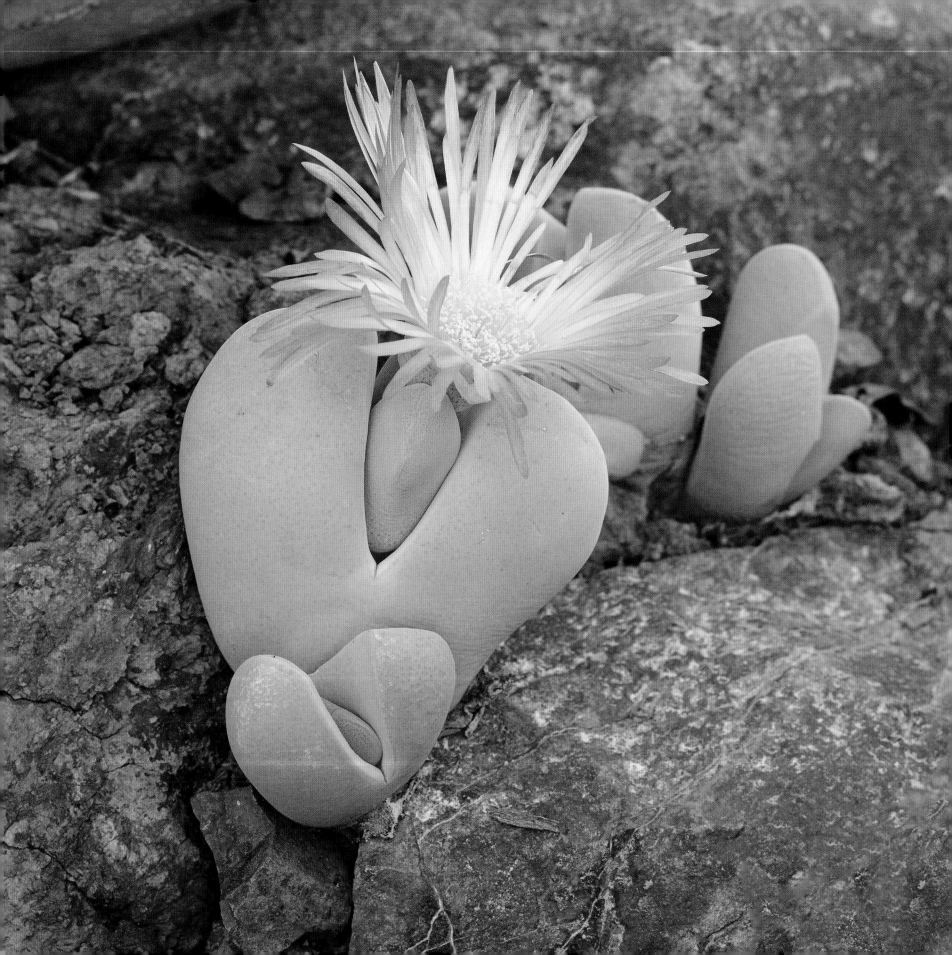

Aloinopsis rubrolineata—a cold-tolerant, pebble-textured ice plant from South Africa—originates from a place with no winter rain. It needs perfect drainage in Ruth's winter-wet climate. ◄

The entire plant body of *Cheiridopsis* is reduced to fused pairs of leaves. The pale blue-green form sports a bright yellow daisy flower and looks perfectly at home in the rock crevice. ◄ ◄

FLOWERS AND FOLIAGE

Flowers add color, drama, and softness to even the driest garden. Ruth's childhood fascination with flowers carried over into her garden. As the space has matured, so has its palette of blooms. It includes ice plants that cover themselves in bright blooms, wildflowers that sow themselves in every bare spot, and plenty of blooming shrubs.

ICE PLANTS

In the early years of planting the dry garden, Ruth relied heavily on ice plants to get big hits of color. When the ice plants bloom each spring, the garden is ablaze with some of the brightest, most neon shades of red, yellow, orange, and pink. Ruth used a lot of *Lampranthus*, *Cephalophyllum*, and *Delosperma*. These ground covers or low-growing shrubs are some of the most brilliant and reliable bloomers in the succulent world, and useful plants for the edge of borders and beds.

Ice plants with shockingly bright blooms.

Lampranthus aurantiacus. ▲

Cephalophyllum diversiphyllum. ▶

Cheiridopsis rostrata. ◄

Lampranthus spectabilis. ▲

Drosanthemum micans. ▼

ALOE

Ruth's garden is perhaps most famous for its diversity of aloe plants. Their fleshy-leaved structural rosettes captivated Ruth, but the plants are also noteworthy for their reliable yearly blooms in bright reds, oranges, and yellows. While they are known as winter bloomers, Brian's deep dive into collecting and breeding means that from winter through summer there is always an aloe in bloom in the garden.

With more than 500 species, aloes range from miniature to tree form, and many check in at hip height. Every aloe is perennial and polycarpic, meaning each plant flowers annually without dying. They are found in much of sub-Saharan Africa, from the southern tip into the Arabian Peninsula, as well as Madagascar. They vary greatly in their growing conditions, from bone dry to tropical forests. Aloes hailing from regions with low levels of precipitation and high levels of aridity are incredibly drought tolerant, and those are the ones in Ruth's collection. Sunbirds, narrow-beaked nectar-feeding birds not found in the Americas, pollinate their tubular flowers. In the Americas, hummingbirds often do the job.

While there are some aloes from winter-wet climates along the west coast of South Africa, most hail from summer-rainfall climates. But aloes are forgiving. They will take water whenever it comes and are very unfussy. However, that forgiving nature extends only one way, as species adapted to summer-dry climates will not tolerate persistent summer humidity.

Aloe 'Creamsicle' (*A. ferox* × *A. arborescens*) exhibits structural and floral appeal.

White fuzzy flowers of *Aloe tomentosa*.

Brian started *Aloe plicatilis*, the largest in the garden, from seed in 1982. Native to South Africa, it has smooth bark and fanned leaves, and it needs winter rainfall and protection from frost. In its native habitat it grows taller than wide. It is wider than tall in North America, but no one is sure why. ▲

Varying heights of an *Aloe* hybrid (*A. ferox* × *A. arborescens*) make for a layered look. ◄

A lovely clump of *Aloe arborescens* explodes in bloom. ◄ ◄

Similar to agaves, aloes hold year-round structure in the garden. As with her collection of *Yucca*, Ruth practiced wildscaping with many types of *Aloe*, leaving their dead, persistent leaves attached to their trunks to become another layer of sculptural appeal. *Aloe* is an excellent, forgiving choice for a home garden.

Aloe hybrid (*A. striata* × *A. reynoldsii*). ▲ / ▶ ▶

Aloe striata hybrid. ◄

Aloe buhrii hybrid. ▲

Aloe buhrii. ▶

Aloe reynoldsii hybrid. ◀

These aloes stay small. *Aloe microstigma* has red leaves, while the blue ones belong to *Aloe glauca*.

Aloe microstigma and *A. glauca.*

Aloe glauca. ▲

Aloe burgersfortensis. ◄

Aloe speciosa.

Aloe 'Creamsicle' (*A. ferox* × *A. arborescens*) is one of Brian's hybrids.

Aloe maculata. ▲

Aloe capitata var. *quartziticola* has a very strange flower. Other aloes bloom from bottom to top. *Aloe capitata* has its own way—it is not strictly top to bottom, but it definitely is not bottom to top. ▲ ▲

This aloe came from UC Berkeley marked *Aloe capitata*. The garden staff has since categorized it as *A. capitata* var. *quartziticola* × *A. cryptopoda*. ▶

Breeding your own

If you want to see hybridiziation take place in your own collection, start plants from seed. Species of *Gasteria* are easiest, followed by aloes and agaves. Cactus can be trickier. Place the seeds in a mix that is three-quarters pumice and one-quarter potting soil, and keep it moist through germination. You can place the pot inside a plastic bag to ensure the moisture remains high, but this increases the chances of fungal infections. And be careful: this is an addictive habit, and you may find yourself running out of room in your greenhouse or protected spots in the garden.

Aloe microstigma. ▲

Aloe wickensii. ◄

EUPHORBIA

One of Ruth's all-time favorite groups is *Euphorbia* because of its diversity of forms and flowers. Sometimes known as spurges, euphorbias are native to many parts of the world. The genus is among the most diverse on the planet, ranging from cactus-like types to herbaceous garden plants to the poinsettia. The succulent ones are concentrated in Madagascar, Africa, the Arabian Peninsula, and India. The family includes around 300 genera and more than 2000 species; of these, about 870 are considered succulent. All euphorbias secrete a caustic white sap that is toxic to humans and pets. Another defining characteristic of *Euphorbia* is its unique flower structure, known as a cyathium, which has fused bracts that form a cup around a much-reduced flower. There are glands around the rim of the cup that vary greatly; some look like cushions, while others resemble miniature hands with little fingers.

Euphorbia echinus, one of two Moroccan species in the garden, has spiny edges.

A patch of *Euphorbia resinifera*, the other Moroccan native, makes a compact mound of many cylindrical stems. It is a relatively hardy species. ▲

Ruth planted *Euphorbia* 'Zig Zag', a hybrid of *E. pseudocactus* and *E. grandicornis*, which shows off its variegated candelabra and spiny stems. ◄

Situated under a palm for protection, *Euphorbia tetragona*, a tender South African tree, forms a large trunk with many vertical branches. ▶

Three types of *Euphorbia* play next to one another. At the top, *E. inermis* var. *huttonae* is covered in white stubs of old flower stalks. Bluish *E. myrsinites*, a broad-leafed variety, grows in the middle. A spontaneous hybrid Medusoid type radiates at the bottom.

Originally planted by Ruth, *Euphorbia myrsinites* now readily reseeds itself in the garden, creating radiating stems of spirally arranged triangular blue-gray leaves. This hardy variety is unbothered by extremes, handling temperatures as low as –20°F, extreme summer heat, and little irrigation. ◄

Self-seeded *Euphorbia* hybrids (mixes of *E. esculenta* and other Medusoid types). ▲

Ruth planted spiraling Medusoid *Euphorbia*, including *E. inermis* and *E. esculenta*. They reseed readily from explosively released seeds, so most of those in the garden are spontaneous hybrids. ▶

Ruth began using euphorbias by planting several species together in the garden in order to study them. In bed 5, she shows off a few hardy varieties. *Euphorbia esculenta* is a Medusoid type, named for its snake-like arms that spiral out from the center. The plant is surprisingly cold tolerant and resistant to root rot, so it adapted well to the garden and has reseeded freely. Nearby is *Euphorbia tetragona*, a columnar variety that, as the name suggests, has four ridged sides. Spilling from every side of the bed is *Euphorbia myrsinites*, a softer blue-green variety that has pointed leaves and creates a touch of lushness. Although once an intentional planting, it has thrived in the garden and found itself so at home that it shows up everywhere, almost like a weed.

Euphorbia myrsinites is a great choice to repeat in a dry garden because it can handle both heat and drought. Whorled blue-green leaves trail away from a central stem in a bowl-shaped pattern, topped with clusters of chartreuse flowers. It is the ultimate filler, perfect for bare spots between plants, bed edges, and containers. It will gently cascade over the edges of retaining walls or pots.

Green-stemmed *Euphorbia antisyphilitica*, lined with pink and white flowers along the stalks, sits in front of blooming *Senna nemophila*. ▶

Euphorbia horrida, one of Ruth's favorites, has a white stem and red-purple flowers. ◀

Many euphorbias look suspiciously similar to ribbed globular or short columnar cactus. The similarity is so striking, it would be hard to distinguish between the plants if they were not growing side by side. Ruth loved this type of synchronicity. She devoted bed 5 to examining cactus and their lookalike *Euphorbia* equivalents. Indigenous to harsh deserts in opposite hemispheres, both form lots of spines and grow in stumpy shapes. The differences are apparent when you examine the spines. On a true cactus, each cluster of spines is composed of individual spikes emanating from one point, or areole. But while types of *Euphorbia* appear to have spines, they are never clustered, like those of a cactus. A euphorbia might have a hardened peduncle that becomes a spine, a horned rib along its edge, or one spine that branches. This example of convergent evolution—in which organisms evolve similar traits as a result of having to adapt to similar environments but in different parts of the world—fascinated Ruth. Cactus are the only plants with areoles. Both cactus-like *Euphorbia* and cactus, native to different continents, evolved to be similarly sharp, but they use different botanical features to get the job done.

Many of these cactus-like euphorbias are pushing the limits on tenderness. Give them protection in the winter or grow them in mild-winter climates. Use them as specimen plants against a softer background, such as *Xanthorrhoea*.

Euphorbia grandicornis grows in the corner of the propagation greenhouse. Ruth loved this plant and kept trying to grow it outside, but it is not hardy enough to survive.

An up-close view of *Euphorbia grandicornis*. ◄

Euphorbia stellispina looks like a cactus, but its branch spines give it away. ►

GASTERIA

When not in flower, you might be apt to confuse certain types of *Gasteria*, succulents native to South Africa, with an aloe or even an agave. They are famous for their leaves, which are often spotted, flecked, or sharp on the edges. But in bloom, a gasteria is hard to confuse with anything else. Its attractive flowers dangle individually from a thin stem, and are usually bright orange, pink, or coral, often with contrasting ivory or green mouths. They look like hanging stomachs—hence the name—and they produce nectar, making them hummingbird magnets. *Gasteria acinacifolia* is an especially large variety that makes a great impact if planted en masse with a backdrop of larger agaves.

Purple coarse-textured leaves of *Gasteria batesiana* 'Barberton'. ▲

A patch of *Gasteria acinacifolia*, with arching flowering stalks, makes a dazzling display. ►

Pink bottlebrush flowers of *Grevillea petrophiloides* catch the late afternoon light.

South African *Leucospermum* 'Pink Ribbons' sports an almost alien-like bloom in late winter. ◄

Leucadendron 'Little Bit' features creamy blossoms with yellow and green centers. ▶

PROTEA

Hailing from Australia and South Africa, plants in Proteaceae are some of the showiest blooms in the garden. They are great year-round shrubs and perfect as foundation plantings, as they burst into unexpectedly otherworldly blooms in late winter. These plants are endlessly useful in landscape design and come in a range of sizes and heights. Use them massed together to make a larger impact. They prove that dry can still be lush.

The trick to keeping proteas happy in the garden is to adjust the soil pH to be acidic rather than alkaline. There are two ways to do this. For quick blasts, add chelated iron, which breaks down quickly. For longer-term adjustments, add granulated sulfur each spring. It takes three to four months for bacteria to break it down into a mild sulfuric acid. Once that happens, the plants can take up their own nutrients. Water is generally alkaline and flushes the soil, so the more you have to water (such as in the heat of Walnut Creek), the more you need to adjust the pH. Correcting soil pH is more important than adding fertilizer. Keep in mind that only protea relatives need this treatment—all other Australian and South African plants do just fine with alkaline soil and fertilizer.

Terrestrial bromeliads offer bright summer blooms. A clump of *Dyckia* in the foreground sends up orange inflorescences, while those in back are more yellow.

TERRESTRIAL BROMELIADS

Terrestrial bromeliads are the orphans of the bromeliad family. With their fabulous leaf colors and markings, plus wildly bright blooms, bromeliads are incredibly popular. But traditional bromeliads are too tender for anywhere except the mildest winter areas—we have much better luck with the terrestrial forms. We can put them right in the ground; they are hardy and tough. Rosettes paired with bright flowers are a win in the garden. Small dyckias are far and away the best suited for a home garden. Many types of *Puya* simply grow too large, while *Deuterocohnia*, while small, are sharp to the point of inhospitable. They are not a fun ground cover to groom.

A purple *Dyckia* hybrid. ▲

A *Dyckia* hybrid. ◄

The rigid rosette forms of *Dyckia*, often lined along the margins with some of the meanest spines, make these plants a great choice for the landscape. There are more than 120 species, all native to South America, most of which are from southern Brazil down to Argentina. In the wild, they are found among rocks in warm, sunny areas ranging from the coast to the foothills of the Andes. These plants are quite tough; they can withstand drought, neglect, and cold.

Making up for their dreadful spines, all dyckias bear bright flowers in spring and summer. There are some yellow-flowered dyckias, but orange is really their color. And although the flowers are not giants, they are magnetic to hummingbirds. The plants are not monocarpic, meaning they keep growing after flowering.

A clump of *Puya coerulea* var. *monteroana* shoots up flower stalks behind the trunk of an oak that used to live in the garden.

When Ruth was first growing her collection, very few dyckias were available. Besides a few silver-leafed types, she was able to get her hands on only somewhat boring-leaved green *Dyckia brevifolia* and equally ho-hum *D. encholirioides*. But then came the dyckia explosion in the 1980s. Several hybridizers, most notably Bill Baker from the San Fernando Valley, released hundreds of different colors and varieties. "Suddenly there were purple ones! Silver ones! Super-toothy ones," Brian said. Ruth loved them all and planted many in the garden. But to date, no adequate book on dyckias exists, and it is hard to track down encyclopedic information.

As more and more gardeners begin creating vignettes of small fleshy-leaved succulents, they will likely turn to dyckias, which are the special sauce to this combination. Their form is pleasingly geometric, but their texture—flat leaves and sharp spines—takes any composition to the next level.

Species of *Puya*, another terrestrial bromeliad from South America, have leaves that range from grassy to sword-like but are always well armed. Although they are organized in a rosette form, they usually read as large clumps of silver or green leaves whose individual heads are far less ornamental than those of a dyckia. Unlike succulents, puyas have no internal water storage tissue. Their leaves look almost fuzzy because of trichomes, specialized cells that can absorb water and nutrients out of the air.

In the garden, try *Puya alpestris* for its silver mounds that add height to the back of a vignette. The blue-green flower is otherworldly. Or, use *P. coerulea* in a mass planting. The attractive rosettes are ghost white in color. Purple flowers burst upward in spring atop ascending stalks.

Puya berteroniana has giant metallic-looking flowers. Brian noted that no one thinks they are real. ▼

Notice the built-in bird perches of *Puya berteroniana*. A South American bird pollinates every puya in the wild; in Ruth's garden, any available birds and bees do the job. ▲

Unlike in a dyckia, a puya rosette is monocarpic (it dies after flowering), but because it grows in clumps you are not likely to notice the disappearance of any one rosette. Their saving grace is their flowers. The colors are almost bizarre, from purple-black to blue-green. The absolute showstopper is *Puya berteroniana*, with its metallic turquoise flowers. The inflorescence requires birds for pollination. *Puya berteroniana* produces wide-open blooms and built-in perches on which birds can rest while they feed.

Comprising many tight rosettes, *Deuterocohnia* is pretty, but deadly sharp.

While not noteworthy for flowers like the other terrestrial bromeliads in Ruth's collection, *Deuterocohnia* (formerly *Abromeitiella*) deserves a mention. These miniature super spiny rosettes form what look like thick, mossy mounds. They also have a distinctly under-the-sea feeling, like something you might encounter in a coral reef. These plants are extremely sharp, so use them with caution and only in an area where you will not have to brush against them. They are handsome at the edge of a border or tucked around a larger plant, like an agave or a yucca.

Deuterocohnia mounding like it
is at the bottom of the sea.

South African *Phylica pubescens* is fussy one: it is difficult to propagate, needs perfect drainage, and dies if overwatered. ◄

Amid more structural aloe, *Melinis nerviglumis* moves in the breeze. ►

THE SOFTER SIDE

Ruth's garden is sharp, and filled with needles, spines, and rough edges. However, there are also bulbs, wildflowers, and grasses that reveal a softer side of the collection. Unlike so many of Ruth's plants, which offer year-round structure, several of these softer plants are alive seasonally, adding texture or color for a few days or weeks before dying or going dormant again until the following year. This palette adds delicious texture to the sharp plants and heightens their forms.

Once the main bed of winter-blooming aloes has finished its display, an eruption of ruby grass (*Melinis nerviglumis*) takes center stage. One of the most striking of all ornamental grasses, this South African native has blue-green foliage that grows into clumps measuring around one foot tall and wide. In fall the foliage turns shades of purple-red, but the real show is in late summer, when it blooms pink seedheads held more than a foot above clumps. The entire clump, but especially the flowers, blows in the wind and catches the light as it changes, creating a strong sense of movement in the bed.

Purple-flowered *Polygala virgata* softens a patch of cactus.

Its leaves look like they were bitten by a shark, so *Agave xylonacantha* used to be known as *A. carchariodonta*, the genus for a great white shark. South African *Bulbine* is the perfect companion for an agave. It is also perfectly dry, but adds deeper green, feathery texture and hits of orange and yellow flowers. ▲

The sweet, dainty blooms of *Bulbinella nutans*. ◄

South African *Bulbine* and its relative, *Bulbinella,* both have yellow flowers (with slight differences). They appreciate the same dry conditions as the plants they grow among in Ruth's collection, but they are more lush, dark green, and soft, with bright flowers. A bulbine almost always looks like a succulent, reminiscent of a small aloe, with leaves ranging from pencil-like to broad. A bulbinella grows all through the winter as nondescript green clumps, then bursts into bloom in February and March. Afterward, it dies back to a corm-like base underground to re-emerge with winter rain. The less succulent leaves are wrapped in a fibrous layer.

Dark green *Agave shawii* holds structure in an otherwise soft bed of buckwheat, including pink-flowered *Eriogonum grande* var. *rubescens* and off-white-flowered *Eriogonum nudum*. In front, a dwarf ephedra looks almost grass-like with petite dark green stems. ◄

In the (mostly) California natives bed, *Iris douglasiana* finishes its spring bloom with orange California poppies and silvery *Tanacetum ptarmiciflorum* in the background. The odd aloe is not a native, but it picks up the orange poppies nicely. ►

CALIFORNIA NATIVES

In the part of the garden farthest from her home, where the beds meet Bancroft Road (formerly a two-lane road and now a busy thoroughfare), Ruth experimented with California natives. While she always insisted that she did not choose her palette to prove any point about saving water, but rather for their pleasing forms, her foray into Mediterranean-climate dry plants—not half as showy or freakish as cactus—calls that into question. It is not entirely clear what aspect of these plants caught Ruth's attention. It is likely their burst of blooms each spring, but there is no denying that Ruth's garden contains some of the best examples of how to garden in a summer-dry climate. Some of these plants go dormant in summer, but each fall, rain permitting, they begin to grow and fill in the most herbaceous part of the garden, and by spring this back corridor is awash in the bright blooms of native orange and cream poppies, pink and purple *Penstemon* (which Ruth ordered left and right), bright yellow buckwheat, blue and purple *Salvia* with woolly blue curls, and golden-yellow *Fremontodendron*. And just when you think you've found the thornless part of the garden, be especially careful around *Colletia paradoxa*, a South American shrub related to native Californian *Ceanothus* (which is how it found its way into this part of the garden). Its blooms smell of vanilla, and it has clawed leaves that resemble chicken feet and dig their way into your skin. Ryan Penn has a particular passion for California natives and has introduced many more, including more salvias, brodiaeas (a purple-flowering bulb), closely related *Dichelostema*, more *Dudleya*, and, sharing in Ruth's initial foray, plenty of *Penstemon*.

Tulipa saxatilis intermixed with *Brunsvigia josephinae*. ▲

In the California native bed, California poppies self-seed among structural spiky blue rosettes of *Hesperoyucca whipplei*, which originates from the central coast of California to Baja. ◄

Incorporating natives into your home garden does not mean it will turn into an unkempt habitat garden. Try using *Ceanothus* as a hedge, either clipped or a little wilder. Along a fence or wall, espalier *Garrya elliptica* or *Fremontodendron*. Grow a meadow of *Carex pansa* with dudleyas interspersed for structure. Mix white-flowered romneyas in liberally with Australian shrubs and trees, and add *Salvia clevelandii* for the best-scented foliage around.

No bed boasts as much ephemeral softness as the area of (mostly) California natives. In spring, self-seeding California poppies (*Eschscholzia californica*) grow everywhere. Orange blooms sit atop blue-green foliage. As soon as they fade, buckwheats (*Eriogonum*) are hot on their trail, exploding into white, pink, and yellow branched flowers on clumps of silver-green foliage.

Agave shawii anchors this view. St. Catherine's lace (*Eriogonum giganteum*) grows all around it with the tallest clump on the right; chocolate daisy (*Berlandiera lyrata*), native to the Great Plains, blooms in the foreground; and blue sticks of *Ephedra equisetina* stand in the back. This is not a native ephedra, but Ruth planted it here to be near other California native types.

From left to right, a canopy of *Prosopis glandulosa*, *Brahea armata*, and *Pinus edulis*.

TREES

The trees in Ruth's garden were planted to provide shade for sun-sensitive succulents, rather than as features of the collection, but they have become important components to the success of the design and the staff have added more over time. Combining planting islands with large structured plants or trees has a long-term payoff. They have grown tall enough to create walkways that feel enclosed and to conceal parts of the garden, transforming those mounded beds into outdoor rooms and creating a delightful tension of never knowing what will come around the next bend. Also, as the trees have matured they have created a large number of shade situations—east exposure (key for plants that dislike the full-blasting afternoon sun), dappled light, and lots of microclimates for staff to play with.

If you already have trees, make them work for you by incorporating them into a landscape. Established trees are often the least water-taxing features of a landscape, plus they offer shade, habitat, and a cooling effect to the overall area. You will find out very quickly if you can plant under their canopy by taking a trowel underneath. If the soil is filled with masses of feeder roots, you will not be able to dig. Also, some trees have leaf litter or allelopathic compounds that make the understory a tough place to grow. But if you use a tree for dappled light, be aware of the directional nuance. The north side offers the most shade, while the south side will be sunnier. The east side offers morning light—plant love this—while the western side is exposed to the hottest afternoon sun.

Brahea armata makes it easy to understand why palms are often called the ultimate foliage plants. ◄

A wall of palms. From left to right: green *Trithrinax campestris*, blue *Trithrinax campestris*, and *Chamaerops humilis. Yucca carnerosana* acts as the exclamation point in the center, while at ground level dyckia hybrids burst into two shades of orange blooms. ◄ ◄

Ruth loves palms. Single-trunk types add vertical drama without taking up much space (Brian referred to them as the exclamation points of the garden). Clumping varieties create huge screenings, serving as outdoor room dividers. Palms are a massively large group, with more than 200 genera and 2600 species, native to areas ranging from rainforests to deserts. Ruth sought out the low-water varieties for her collection, knowing they would thrive in her climate without breaking Phil's rule of no new wells.

Native to northern Baja, *Brahea armata*, a single trunked-palm, is among the most dry-adapted. As the silver leaves die, the plant retains its foliage. This feature might be removed in a more manicured garden, but Ruth was far more interested in observing how the plant changes over time. If the thatch is removed, the plant almost appears naked. This cold-hardy palm can survive to 15°F.

One could get lost in the geometry of *Trithrinax campestris*. Each petiole makes room for the next, revealing a gentle lean of each leaf, while fibers around the base of the leaves have patterns and look like burlap macramé. ◄ / ▲

This is the perfect vantage point to compare a clump of *Trithrinax campestris* in the foreground with *Washingtonia filifera* looming tall in the distance. ▼

Native to northern Baja and into the Coachella valley, *Washingtonia filifera* is California's native fan palm. This oasis plant loves water and will make the most of a small amount in an otherwise extremely dry area. It has adapted to survive dry summers and wetter winters. Ruth planted four (now down to three; one was lost to diamond scale fungus) in a staggered line, just as one might find them outside Palm Springs. They now tower more than 40 feet tall, with massive thatch skirts that lay down in the most even, perfectly arranged manner.

From savannas of northern Argentina, *Trithrinax campestris*, a low-growing palm, experiences summer flooding and winter drought in its native habitat, but does just fine in Ruth's garden. This is one of the sharpest palms, evolved to deter giant herbivores before the Ice Age. While it is usually a clumping variety, it occasionally grows as a single trunk. Ruth has both.

Chamaerops humilis and blue *Trithrinax campestris.*

Native to the Italian Riviera, Sicily, Tunisia, Morocco, and Spain, *Chamaerops humilis* is the only palm native to Europe, and it is perfectly suited to Ruth's dry summers and wetter winters. While it will survive severe drought, it is happiest with regular water. This petite, well-formed tree is the best candidate to add to a home garden.

Butia capitata has a
decorative trunk and arching,
feathery leaves.

Ruth's valuable *Jubaea chilensis* stands in the far west corner of the garden with its fat trunk and distinctly upright leaf canopy. ▲

The swollen trunk of *Brachychiton rupestris* is a fan favorite in the garden. ◄

Known as the jelly palm, South American *Butia capitata* is among the few ornamental palms that can grow in Northern California and also make delicious fruit. This is a particularly cold-hardy palm, well adapted to coastal environments as well as inland. Although it is happiest with regular water, it will also withstand droughts. It grows in sun or shade.

Valued at around $30,000, Ruth's Chilean wine palm (*Jubaea chilensis*) is the most valuable plant in her collection. This slow-growing, fat-trunked, Mediterranean-climate palm is a highly prized status symbol, although it is doubtful

Ruth liked it for that reason. She got this specimen in the late 1970s from a neighbor. It is hardy to 10°F and tolerates drought, and it has stayed happy for almost 40 years.

Ruth's garden holds a collection of trees adapted to dry climates. A favorite was the Queensland bottle tree (*Brachychiton rupestris*). This Australian native forms a bulbous trunk to use as its personal water tank. Ruth planted several throughout the garden. The largest one swelled so much that it lifted up the ground beneath it, creating a mound of soil. Eager to experiment, Ruth treated this mound as a new planting bed, filling it with *Parodia* cactus and *Eriogonum*.

Exfoliating bark of *Manzanita* 'Ruth Bancroft'. ▲

Pinus edulis, one of Lester's original plantings, frames the pond, just out of sight in the foreground. ▶

One by one, all the California-native manzanita trees that Ruth planted in the garden died because of lack of proper drainage. Then a spontaneous seedling popped up and has persisted in the garden for decades. By midsummer, its red bark exfoliates beautifully.

While pine trees conjure images of cold mountain regions, a number of them are native to Mediterranean regions and arid mountain ranges, with the most diversity in Mexico. Lester's original contributions of three pines are perfect examples of species that fit into a dry garden and add tall, vertical layers. The Rocky Mountain bristlecone pine (*Pinus aristata*) is thought to be one of the longest-living trees in the world, with some clocking in at 5000 years old. Ruth's specimen, planted in the early 1970s, is considered a baby. It has not yet made a full-sized cone. Ruth also has a pinyon pine (*P. edulis*), native to the Rocky Mountains and northern Mexico, along with a single-leaf pinyon pine (*P. monophylla*), native to the American West and Baja. All three contribute a rugged feel to the garden.

At the end of the path stands tall *Pinus monophylla*. An aloe hybrid blooms on the left side of the path, and *Puya berteroniana* forms a silver clump of leaves on the right.

Parkinsonia aculeata in full springtime bloom.

Beautiful green-barked palo verde (*Parkinsonia aculeata*) anchors the space across from the arching bed 6. A common fixture in the southwest desert, this tree needs heat and dislikes cool, coastal conditions. In the Southwest, it blooms in late winter or early spring, just on the cusp of unbearable heat. There's a full four- to five-month delay of the heat in Walnut Creek, and Ruth's palo verde does not bloom until June. The tree holds year-round interest with green bark, a feature caused by photosynthesizing within the outer layer of bark.

Chilopsis provides dappled light for columnar *Oreocereus pseudofossulatus. Dasylirion* grows in the middle of the trunk, and *Deuterocohnia* mounds below. ◄

Prosopis bursts into bright green foliage, delicately shading two agaves. *Pinus edulis* grows in the foreground. ►

Offering the perfect amount of dappled shade for other plants to grow underneath, nurse trees in the garden include mountain mahogany (*Cercocarpus*), mesquite (*Prosopis*), and *Chilopsis*. Southwestern *Chilopsis* has incredible flower production, and in winter the sinuous branches make a nice silhouette against the sky.

Among her trees from Down Under, Ruth experimented with *Eucalyptus* from the very start, and it continues to be an important feature of the garden. As a whole, eucalyptus trees get a bad rap in the Bay Area for being invasive, disease prone, and highly flammable. But the genus is large, and there are smaller forms well adapted to the Northern California climate. They have pretty foliage and sometimes produce big flowers, they need next to no water, and they offer dappled light to plants growing below.

Although somewhat straggly as a tree, *Eucalyptus caesia* is extremely dry-adapted and boasts pink puffy flowers in winter. ▲

Eucalyptus preissiana, a shrub rather than a tree, is notable for leathery blue leaves and small caps, which are actually fused petals. ◄

Eucalyptus kitsoniana, a Lester contribution, still stands tall in the garden with gorgeous exfoliating bark. ◄ ◄

Acacia cognata 'Cousin Itt' is remarkably dark green for being such a dry-adapted plant. ▲

Weeping *Acacia pendula* rubs shoulders with the white blossoms of *Romneya coulteri*. ◄

Sitting almost invisible for most of the year, *Acacia merinthophora* shows off delicate yellow puffs of flowers for just a few weeks each year. ◄ ◄

Ruth planted many different acacias in her garden, some from Australia and some from other parts of the world. A specimen of *Acacia baileyana* stood for a long time until it became too straggly and was removed. When Chilean *Acacia caven* died, the wood was so beautiful that Ruth had a number of local artisans turn it into bowls and other objects.

The garden staff keeps adding more acacias. *Acacia cognata* 'Cousin Itt', released in 2010, forms feathery, evergreen mounds, eventually reaching 2 to 3 feet tall and 4 to 6 feet wide. The plant adds a pop of verdant lushness to dry gardens, as it does in Ruth's. *Acacia merinthophora* stands unassuming all year except for two weeks in March, when it explodes into small, round yellow blooms that seem to be floating in midair, with the lacy, delicate foliage barely visible. *Acacia pendula*, a handsome weeping species with silvery blue-gray long, narrow leaves, will eventually reach 25 feet tall by 15 feet wide.

EPILOGUE

Growing with the Garden

There is something so beautiful and touching about Ruth aging alongside her garden.

She allowed the plants to express themselves fully—growing shaggy or imperfect—while they, in turn, gave her endless inspiration to express herself and engage in plant-driven design so different from anything surrounding her at the time. With curiosity as her compass, she created a garden that would eventually become a model we look to for sustainability and as a reflection of regional appropriateness.

While we cannot know what has kept Ruth engaged well past the centenarian mark, it seems certain that the garden has something to do with it. For someone as intellectually inquisitive as Ruth, plants were an excellent place to take a dive. If we look closely, plants are endlessly engaging. Her lists of varieties to collect never grew smaller, her greenhouse shelves never emptied, and she was never short on a new group to study.

Ruth, age 106.

And if we are patient, the payoff is even bigger. It is so easy to walk through Ruth's garden—with sky-high *Washingtonia filifera*, narrow walks of upright columnar cactus, giant agaves, and shaggy yuccas—and to think that it appeared fully mature; that large equipment craned in certain plants and a giant crew executed a careful design. But that could not be further from the truth. It is almost beyond comprehension that the garden was hand planted, tiny plant by tiny plant, by a woman who did not even wear gardening gloves. She was just following her curiosity to learn. What persistence!

With climate change on the horizon, we are faced with the opportunity to channel the Ruth in all of us. Without knowing how it will all turn out, can we challenge ourselves to be adventurous in our plant choices, attentive to climatic cues, undaunted by failure, and contented by our gardens? Just imagine what might be possible from the procurement of one innocent-looking rosette.

As the sun sets in the west, needles of this opuntia glow in the backlight. At the base, old paddles have hardened into a bark-like protective layer.

METRIC CONVERSIONS

inches	cm
½	1.3
1	2.5
2	5.1
3	7.6
4	10
5	13
6	15
7	18
8	20
9	23
10	25

feet	m
1	0.3
2	0.6
3	0.9
4	1.2
5	1.5
6	1.8
7	2.1
8	2.4
9	2.7
10	3
20	6
30	9
40	12
50	15
100	30
1000	300

SOURCES AND SUGGESTIONS FOR FURTHER READING

Baldwin, Debra Lee. 2007. *Designing with Succulents*. Portland, OR: Timber Press.

Baldwin, Debra Lee. 2013. *Succulents Simplified: Growing, Designing, and Crafting with 100 Easy-Care Varieties*. Portland, OR: Timber Press.

Bancroft, Ruth. "The Ruth Bancroft Garden in Walnut Creek, California: Creation in 1971, and Conservation," an oral history conducted in 1991 and 1992 by Suzanne Riess, Regional Oral History Office, The Bancroft Library, University of California, Berkeley, 1993, digitalassets.lib.berkeley.edu/roho/ucb/text/bancroft_ruth.pdf. Unless otherwise noted, all quotations from Ruth Bancroft come from this source.

Bornstein, Carol and David Fross. 2011. *Reimagining the California Lawn: Water-conserving Plants, Practices, and Designs*. Los Olivos, CA: Cachuma Press.

Brenzel, Kathleen Norris. 2015. *Sunset Western Garden Book of Easy-Care Plantings*. New York: Time Inc. Books.

Calhoun, Scott. 2012. *The Gardener's Guide to Cactus: The 100 Best Paddles, Barrels, Columns, and Globes*. Portland, OR: Timber Press.

Dickey, Page. 2015. *Outstanding American Gardens—25 Years of the Garden Conservancy*. New York: Abrams Books.

Harlow, Nora. 2004. *Plants and Landscapes for Summer-Dry Climates of the San Francisco Bay Region*. East Bay Municipal Utility District.

Horvath, Brent. 2014. *The Plant Lover's Guide to Sedums*. Portland, OR: Timber Press.

Matthews, Lewis J. 2002. *Protea Book: A Guide to Cultivated Proteaceae*. Portland, OR: Timber Press.

Ogden, Scott and Lauren Springer Ogden. 2011. *Waterwise Plants for Sustainable Gardens: 200 Drought-Tolerant Choices for All Climates*. Portland, OR: Timber Press.

Rubin, Greg and Lucy Warren. 2013. *The California Native Landscape: The Homeowner's Design Guide to Restoring Its Beauty and Balance*. Portland, OR: Timber Press.

Schulz, Rudolf. 2011. *Aeonium in Habitat and Cultivation*. Schulz Publishing.

Smith, Gideon F. and Estrela Figueiredo. 2015. *Garden Aloes: Growing and Breeding Cultivars and Hybrids*. Johannesburg: Jacana Media.

Smith, Gideon F. and Braam van Wyk. 2011. *Aloes in Southern Africa*. Parktown North: Penguin Random House South Africa.

Starr, Greg. 2012. *Agaves: Living Sculptures for Landscape and Containers*. Portland, OR: Timber Press.

ACKNOWLEDGMENTS

I'd like to thank the following people and groups for their support in completing this project:

To Adam, for your unwavering support and constant assurance that everything was going to be okay. I'm sorry I made you look at a single *Opuntia* pad for 30 minutes.

To Mom and Dad, for believing in me since I was a wee one shearing your sweet peas to the ground.

To Peggy Northrup and Kathy Brenzel, for support in my day job and for the room to pursue this project.

To Carol Bidnick, for slipping your card into my pocket way back when, and for your long-term patience and support. I'm so glad I know you.

To Juree Sondker, for the perfect amount of nudging, encouragement, and guidance. To Sarah Rutledge for making beauty when I was at wit's end, and to Pat Tompkins for proofreading and poetry.

To all of the staff at the Ruth Bancroft Garden, including Walker Young, Troy McGregor, Ryan Penn, Gretchen Bartzen, Sophie Vidal, and Martin Viveros, for all of your time and access to all of your brains. A particularly heartfelt thank-you to Eileen Hanson for all your archival mastery, logistical coordination, and kindness.

To Dick Turner, for your patience, guidance, and sweet enthusiasm about all things Ruth and her garden. It has been such a treat to consult with you. And thank you to Becky Rice Harrington for offering wise input and sharing shell photographs.

To Ruth's family—Nina and Kathy, for granting me access to family stories and photos, and for your time. And to Suzy Newcomb—you are such a dear friend to Ruth and a total inspiration for the rest of us!

To Robin Stockwell, Ron Lutsko, Jason Dewees, and Daniel Nolan, thank you all heaps and heaps for sharing your plant knowledge and for trekking out to the garden to walk together in person.

To Marion Brenner for spending almost a year's worth of Saturdays with me. I've learned so much from seeing the garden through your eyes. Thank you for finding endless beauty and mystery, even in close-ups. Thank you also for the fresh eggs, peanut butter sandwiches, and all of the homemade jellies.

To Linda Lamb Peters, for being my cheerleader for so many years. You are a talented coworker and a dear friend. Your generosity (and peppermint patties) made this entire project such a delight. I am grateful for your photo-shoot preparedness kit, your keen eye for schmutz, and all the help with photo selection. Your positivity and endless encouragement mean more than I can express. You are the secret weapon in any of my success, and I hope we have a lot more collaboration ahead of us.

To Brian Kemble, it has been an honor to spend time with you in Ruth's garden. There is not another soul in the world as steeped in plant knowledge and as gifted with sharing it enthusiastically as you. This book would not have been possible without you. Thank you for your patience with my maddening inability to spell botanical names.

And to Ruth—I'm so grateful to get to take such a deep dive into your garden. What a beautiful place you've created. I become more inspired and intrigued by it with every visit, and I hope to keep coming back for a long time. Thank you for your hard work. You've created quite a masterpiece, inspired many a soul, and loved many a sharp plant.

Johanna and Ruth in January 2015.

PHOTOGRAPHY CREDITS

Courtesy of the Ruth Bancroft Estate, pages 20, 21 top, 22–27, 29

Courtesy of the Ruth Bancroft Garden, pages 42–46, 49–53, 56 top, 66

Illustrations by Ruth Bancroft, page 68

Becky Harrington, pages 28, 30, 31

Brown Cannon III, page 69

Sibylle V. Olfers, *When the Root Children Wake Up* (*Etwas Von Den Wurzelkindern*), page 21 *Public domain*

All other photographs are by Marion Brenner.

INDEX

Photographs © Marion Brenner except those listed on page 230.

Published in 2016 by Timber Press, Inc.

The Haseltine Building
133 S.W. Second Avenue, Suite 450
Portland, Oregon 97204-3527

timberpress.com

Printed in China

Text and jacket design by Amy Sly

Library of Congress Cataloging-in-Publication Data

Names: Silver, Johanna, author.
Title: The bold dry garden: lessons from the Ruth Bancroft Garden / Johanna
    Silver; photographs by Marion Brenner.
Description: First edition. | Portland, Oregon: Timber Press, 2016. | Includes
    bibliographical references and index.
Identifiers: LCCN 2016001680 | ISBN 9781604696707 (hardcover)
Subjects: LCSH: Landscape gardening—Water conservation. | Xeriscaping. |
    Ruth Bancroft Garden (Walnut Creek, Calif.)
Classification: LCC SB475.83 .S55 2016 | DDC 635.9—dc23 LC record available at
    http://lccn.loc.gov/2016001680

A catalog record for this book is also available from the British Library.